Educational Research for Early Childhood Studies Projects

This accessible book provides a step-by-step guide to carrying out educational research within the context of early years practice. Written by an expert team of authors who have supported many students through their dissertations, it will help you learn the skills necessary to develop ownership and understanding of the research process and successfully complete your dissertation or research project, while maintaining a work–life balance.

The chapters cover all elements of the research process, from advice on choosing a topic and working with your supervisor, to the different research methods you may employ. Ethical considerations and advice on collecting and analysing data and presenting your findings are presented alongside exploratory tasks, proformas and reflective questions, making it a useful companion for dissertation or research project modules. Crucially, the book understands that some undergraduate students may have additional responsibilities and introduces ways to manage workloads alongside caring or work responsibilities.

Aimed at those studying on Early Years Foundation Degrees or Early Childhood Studies courses, this is essential reading for all early years undergraduate students embarking on their first research project.

Jan Gourd is Senior Lecturer at Plymouth Marjon University, UK.

Educational Research for Early Childhood Studies Projects

A Step-by-Step Guide for Student Practitioners

Edited by Jan Gourd

LONDON AND NEW YORK

Designed cover image: © Raimund Koch/Getty Images

First published 2024
by Routledge
4 Park Square, Milton Park, Abingdon, Oxon OX14 4RN

and by Routledge
605 Third Avenue, New York, NY 10158

Routledge is an imprint of the Taylor & Francis Group, an informa business

© 2024 selection and editorial matter, Jan Gourd; individual chapters, the contributors

The right of Jan Gourd to be identified as the author of the editorial material, and of the authors for their individual chapters, has been asserted in accordance with sections 77 and 78 of the Copyright, Designs and Patents Act 1988.

All rights reserved. No part of this book may be reprinted or reproduced or utilised in any form or by any electronic, mechanical, or other means, now known or hereafter invented, including photocopying and recording, or in any information storage or retrieval system, without permission in writing from the publishers.

Trademark notice: Product or corporate names may be trademarks or registered trademarks, and are used only for identification and explanation without intent to infringe.

British Library Cataloguing-in-Publication Data
A catalogue record for this book is available from the British Library

ISBN: 978-0-367-36715-2 (hbk)
ISBN: 978-0-367-36716-9 (pbk)
ISBN: 978-0-429-35093-1 (ebk)

DOI: 10.4324/9780429350931

Typeset in Melior LT Std
by KnowledgeWorks Global Ltd.

Contents

About the authors   vii
Glossary of research terms   ix

Introduction   1

1 Choosing a subject and managing your project   4
  Jan Gourd

2 Working with your supervisor   17
  Miles Smith

3 Methodology and methods   30
  Selina Day

4 Gaining ethical approval   44
  Jonathan Harvey

5 Writing the literature review   57
  Kate Firks

6 Data collection   73
  Jan Gourd

7 Data analysis   84
  Marie Bradwell

8 Recommendations and conclusions   91
  Alison Milner

9 Writing the abstract   105
  Jan Gourd

10 Staying sane *Jan Gourd*	112
11 A student journey *Marie Bradwell*	118
Index	123

About the authors

Jan Gourd

Jan is Senior Lecturer at Plymouth Marjon University and teaches on a wide range of courses. She has a specialism in early years and has previously published on early years policy, flourishing in the early years and thriving as a primary teacher, all with Routledge. Prior to entering higher education teaching, Jan spent 14 years in primary schools as a teacher, deputy teacher and head teacher. In these roles, she established various early years provisions.

Marie Bradwell

Marie is a lecturer at Plymouth Marjon University. Prior to this, Marie worked in early years and education for the past 30 years. She worked in various roles from manager to teaching assistant and with individuals who have special education needs. Her research interests are situated in social policy, early years, children and young people's mental health/illness, active listening and children's rights and using the mosaic approach. She has published on the role of TAs in schools.

Selina Day

Selina is a lecturer in education at the University of St Mark and St John. She draws on her diverse experience within education, including primary and higher education settings. Selina has supervised undergraduate students on a variety of courses. Selina is currently researching her PhD project, which focuses on supporting teachers in discussing controversial issues in religious education sessions using contemporary children's literature.

Kate Firks

Kate has nearly 20 years' experience within both mainstream primary and special education. Her primary research interests are within the fields of disability studies, relating especially to children and young people with autism. She has an additional interest in autoethnographic practice. Kate is a Fellow of the HEA.

Jonathan Harvey

Jonathan is Senior Lecturer in Education and Programme Lead for BA (Hons) Special Educational Needs and Disability Studies at Plymouth Marjon University. He is particularly interested in research that looks at the participation of disabled people in society. He also enjoys engaging in debates around the research process in general. He has previously published 'A Sociological Approach to Acquired Brain Injury and Identity' with Routledge.

Alison Milner

Alison Milner is Senior Lecturer in Education at Plymouth Marjon University. Alison's passion for student-centred pedagogical practices, including personal and professional identity, has led to her PhD research 'A "Creative" Exploration of Academic Identity in College Higher Education'.

Miles Smith

Miles Smith is Associate Dean of Education at Plymouth Marjon University. An experienced teacher, with over 20 years' experience in UK and international contexts, Miles' background is largely in primary education and English language teaching. His research interests are in children's history education, the nature of learning and children's research methodologies.

Glossary of research terms

There are many terms that are often used in research methods course and within the supervision arrangement that students might find baffling and unnecessarily complicated. Whilst we have tried to use simple language or explain terms as we went along, it still seems that a glossary of terms is useful to have and refer to when necessary. This is not an extensive glossary but has been constructed selectively to best represent the core terms most students will encounter.

Action research: Research that helps the practitioner to understand elements of practice within their own setting. The findings can and should inform future development of the setting and the practice within.

Analysis: The use of a systematic method to look at research data and make sense of issues and trends that can be seen.

Case study: An holistic and in-depth look at a specific event/practice within a setting that explores the complexity of the setting as a specific case and that often uses multiple methods to explore differing perspectives.

Constructivism: A position taken that recognises that all knowledge is constructed and set within a specific context. For constructivists, there are many truths and each one is context-dependent.

Dissemination: The sharing of the findings of research.

EECERA: European Early Childhood Education Research Association.

Epistemology: This is the branch of philosophy that asks us to consider what constitutes knowledge for us and how that knowledge is acquired. How do you know what you know?

Ethics: The values and principles that guide research to make sure that no harm is caused by the methodology and methods employed. Ethical procedures calculate risk of harm and require researchers to show how they will mitigate any possible risk.

Focus group: A group interview around a common topic. The group participants can respond to each other as well as to the interviewer's stimulus questions or artefacts. The promotion of discussion is a major feature of this method.

Gate keeper: The person or persons who have the authority to allow access to participants of the research site. This is often the manager or owner of an early years setting or, in the case of schools, the head teacher.

Interview: The method of asking participants to give their opinions or reflections to a set of questions. The questions may be structured or semi-structured or the interview might collect responses to some stimulus material.

Mixed method: A research approach that might include the collection of both qualitative and quantitative data.

Mosaic approach: An approach to research that seeks to use a multimodal approach to data collection to try to make sense of the experience of the participant. The approach is often used when working with young children as multiple perspectives on the experience can be gathered and viewed holistically. The approach is attributed to Clark and Moss (2011).

Observation: A method of gathering data in the research setting. This might be structured according to a schedule or unstructured and gathered via a narrative account.

Ontology: How you view the nature of reality.

Qualitative research: Research that generally uses narrative data that is non-numerical and which relies on an analysis of the context to generate validity. The data is interpreted by the researcher for the reader.

Quantitative research: Research whereby the methods chosen generate numerical data that can generally be displayed in charts and graphs. Numerical data can be analysed using statistical tools.

Questionnaire: A pre-prepared set of questions that are usually answered without the researcher present. Questions can be closed, which allows for the collection of numerical data, or open, which requires a narrative response.

Research project/dissertation: A study often conducted by students in their third year of a degree that requires them to investigate a research question of their own choosing and to write an extended piece on the design, implementation and findings of the study. This is usually approximately 10,000 words for an undergraduate.

Sample: A group selected by the researcher to represent the chosen attributes of participants that will help to answer the research question.

Introduction

This book has been written to support all students of early years practice, but particularly those who are juggling work, job and maybe family. The authors have spent many years teaching early years practitioners on several undergraduate programmes and we are always amazed at the level of commitment that students who are juggling multiple responsibilities bring to their studies. Some students find studying a bit of escapism, whilst others struggle with this added burden of demand on their energy and time. Some struggle with the guilt of the time they spend on this rather than being with their children, helping them with their schoolwork or just being there. We understand the difficulties you face and the competing demands, and as such, we have tried to adopt a pragmatic approach to this text. We hope that it will guide you through your research project and also encourage you to maintain a work–life balance and take care of yourself as well as undertake a successful project.

This is in no way a comprehensive research text. It has never aimed to be. It is a selective and pragmatic text that sets out to guide a student through their project. The authors, amongst them, have supported hundreds of students. We like to think we have encountered most of the issues that arise when supporting you.

Often at the outset, students have grand ideas about the scale and scope of their project, and whilst we want you to be energised and enthused, we also need you to be realistic. You need to be realistic about the timeline in which you must complete the projects, which will probably include review by an ethics panel, which will take time:

- to do the literature review,
- to plan and carry out the research,
- to analyse the findings,
- to write up,
- to meet your supervisor and
- to breathe and maintain your 'normal' life.

It is better to have a simple research design with fewer participants and a simple question(s) than anything too complex. Doing a simple project well will get a better grade than a complex project that runs out of time and it will certainly be less stressful both for you and your supervisor. As such, we are taking a fundamental approach to this book. It will guide you through the basics of research design and data collection. It will guide you through the literature review. We will not offer complex perspectives, which would be necessary for postgraduates. If you are a postgraduate student and found this book then treat this as a refresher as it isn't really going to offer you the depth of perspective that you need.

Researching any aspects of early years practice can be challenging ethically. There is research about the practice from the practitioner's viewpoint, the parents' viewpoint and, importantly, increasing attempts to try to understand the experience from the children's viewpoint. Neoliberal ideology has impacted all areas of early years practice and, as such, it is interesting to challenge the positions in which we find the early years agendas now located. Are parents really consumers of early years services? Are children just to be viewed as economic capital? Can early years practice be reduced to techno rational tick list approaches to ever changing quality agendas? This is the fascinating and complex reality of early years education in England today and it is only by educating practitioners to recognise and challenge these realities of their work that we can challenge the hegemonic 'regimes of truth' (Foucault 1969/1982) that dominate and control what we believe we are supposed to do. Research plays a part in giving practitioners a voice to advocate for themselves and the children and families they work with. Moss (2019) suggests that practitioners need to tell their stories to challenge the dominant discourses of neoliberalism, which he frighteningly makes transparent and optimistically hopes to challenge. To challenge through activism and speaking out. Research is your chance to speak out (Moss 2019).

In Chapter 1, we look at getting started and formulating a working title for your project. The chapter aims to provide some inspiration for the uninspired and some refining for those who are ready to go.

Chapter 2 looks at the centrality of the student–supervisor relationship and how to make this work effectively to your benefit. Sometimes, this relationship doesn't work and there is advice for those situations as well.

Chapter 3 looks at some of the common research methods that students often employ. This is not comprehensive; we have been very selective here, but there are signposts to other texts that you might want to consult if this is not comprehensive enough to meet your needs.

Chapter 4 looks at gaining ethical approval for your study. Students sometimes find this a difficult topic to negotiate and all institutions have different forms and procedures but the principles remain the same. It is worth noting that time spent thinking through the ethical issues and how these will be managed are liable to make the whole project more robust, so please try to think of this as part of the overall project and not just another task that needs to be done.

Chapter 5 considers the literature review and this provides the scaffolding for the project. The literature review can cause you to question or can add further questions to your outline plan. It is important to stay focused and organised during this phase of the process, and Chapter 5 should help you to do that.

Chapter 6 is about the 'doing' part of the research process – the collecting of data. This is where you really need to be pragmatic and limit the amount of data you collect. You simply do not have time to collect a hundred 3,000-word interviews and analyse them all. You would need a team of research assistants to do this in the time span you will have. Here we advise you be realistic but robust in your data collection.

Chapter 7 looks at what you do with the data once you have collected it and how you make sense of the messages that the data presents you with.

Chapter 8 considers how you present and disseminate the results of the study so that your hard work gets the recognition that it deserves and adds to how you and others practice professionally so that real benefits come from the time spent on the study (it would be a waste of human capital else).

Chapter 9 looks at writing the last part, which paradoxically goes at the beginning of the study to inform those who might read it of what knowledge they might gain. That is the writing of the abstract.

In Chapter 10, we look at looking after yourself through the process, and then, finally, in Chapter 11, Marie tells her story of her 'dissi' year.

We also included a glossary of terms as the terms used in research are not always part of everyday language, and those that are may have specific nuances in a research context. We hope that this glossary can act as a reference tool for you when reading research texts.

We hope that this book will help you to see that research can be fun and that planning can alleviate some of the inevitable stress.

Reference

Moss, P. (2019). *Alternative Narratives in Early Childhood: An Introduction for Students and Practitioners* (3rd ed.). Routledge.

1 Choosing a subject and managing your project

Jan Gourd

Introduction

This chapter will look at the importance of choosing a subject that will sustain your interest over an extended period. It will contain exercises to help you decide on what you are interested in and why you are interested in it. You should complete all the exercises as you go through them. We would suggest keeping a research project notebook.

We will take the analogy of a pencil, taking a 'blunt' area and continually sharpening the focus until a workable title for your research project is reached.

There will be advice on 'working titles' and 'final titles' so that you understand that research is a dynamic, not a rigid process. Some of you will find this living with uncertainty very hard. That is normal.

There will also be specific sections on managing your time and achieving work–life balance. We will remind you of the importance of maintaining normality for your family and friends. Throughout, there will be narratives and stories from students just like you who lived through it and survived. They tell their story, warts and all.

Possible areas of interest

What am I interested in?

At some point in your degree, if your degree is honours level (otherwise known as level 6), you will encounter an assessment that requires you to engage in research. Unlike most of the academic work that you have done up until this point, you will not be given a title. You will need to decide on a topic, linked to your course and your final degree title, that you are interested in to sustain a long piece of work, often lasting the whole academic year.

This piece of work is often called an 'Honours Project' or 'Dissertation' and you will be required to research and write between 6000 and 10,000 words on your topic of interest. This work is very individual, and generally, you will be assigned a supervisor but will be expected to be self-motivated to plan, carry out the research and report on your findings. Your supervisor will arrange one-to-one or small group meetings to help you with this. You will find useful advice on working with your supervisor in the next chapter.

Getting started

Often, one of the most difficult aspects for many students is thinking about what they are interested in. We have, until this point, generally led students to develop interests in their chosen field of study. In our institution, we have a module in Year 2 of our courses called 'Research Methods' and this is where we get students thinking about the topics that interest them individually. Often when I do my introductory session on 'Research Methods', the students look alarmed when I say **that they will be deciding what they will be learning and writing about** and that this piece of work often has a significant effect on their final degree grade. They seem alarmed that the cosy days of the tutor, at least in part, designing the investigations/area of study, are over and that they are being released into the academic writing world on their own. They are not, of course, on their own, that is where the supervisor comes in, but this is a significant shift in the teaching and learning arrangement to date. To get you started thinking about your interests, you will find some possibilities discussed in the following. Remember this list is not extensive; it is just to get you thinking!

You might be interested in.

Early years policy

If you are interested in how we come to be where we are in terms of early years practice, then maybe you want to look at a project that looks at how policy has impacted practice, for example, you might want to look at the following:

- The advent of the Early Years Foundation Stage (EYFS)
- How the EYFS has changed practice over the years
- A comparative study of the EYFS and Te Whakiri
- Using the EYFS to plan the curriculum in a day nursery

Each of these would form suitable research projects. The first one '**The advent of the EYFS**' would probably be completed through secondary research or what is sometimes called a **systematic literature review**. Another name for this is a **desk-based study**.

As a student completing this study, you would discuss with your supervisor the time period that you will concentrate on, where in history do we see the antecedents of the EYFS and you might well refine your title to.

The advent of the EYFS from Plowden to 2023 (sharpening the title helps us to keep focused so that we can go into depth on our chosen area).

You would then start your dissertation or project considering how the Plowden Report in 1969 could be considered as an antecedent for the current iteration of the EYFS. How the Conservative government under Margaret Thatcher was the first to start thinking about early years education within a neo-liberal ideology that sought to determine how advancing early years education might be good for the country economically.

If you were to complete this as a study, you would need to make a timeline of all the important policy documents that were published during that time frame and give a critical analysis of the political drivers of each.

You would be searching for the policy documents themselves (an explanation of these as grey literature is given in Chapter 5). You would then also be looking for texts that critiqued those policy documents and that considered the social contexts of each, so you would be searching for books and papers on politics, social history, policymaking and ideology, to name but a few.

If you were interested in '**How the EYFS has changed practice**', you would also probably be looking at some of the themes suggested earlier and you might also decide to do some primary or firsthand research and maybe interview older practitioners about how their practice had changed since the EYFS. More information on interviews is given in Chapter 3.

If you were interested in how other countries provided early years education, then you could do what is called a comparative study. An example of this might be '**A comparative study of the EYFS and Te Whakiri**'. You would probably start this with a discussion of the differing contexts, geographical and political, of England and New Zealand. You would then look at how these contexts impacted the content of the curriculum. This most probably would be a desk-based study unless you had access to practitioners within your chosen comparative country in which case you might wish to send a questionnaire or conduct interviews. This is increasingly possible due to the use of technology and there is a very good book on using digital methods in research called 'Research Methods for Education in the Digital Age' by Savin-Baden and Tombs (2017).

I once had a student who had been working in a nursery in New Zealand for a couple of years and she was still in contact with the practitioners. What she did was to ask her previous colleagues to take photographs of their setting (there were ethical implications here about making sure that children weren't photographed or, if they were, that the appropriate permissions had been obtained; see Chapter 4 for more on the ethical implications of research) and then to describe why things were as they were in the photographs; for example, the resources available, the layout of the nursery, etc. She then did the same at her own nursery and used these pictures in a method called photo-elicitation to analyse and compare practice in the different settings (see Chapter 3 for more on photo-elicitation).

Finally, you might be interested in looking at practice in your own setting and considering '**How the EYFS is used to plan the curriculum in a day nursery in XXXX**'. If you were interested in this, then you would probably be taking a case study approach, that is, you would be looking at one specific setting and how that setting operated the EYFS in the planning stages of provision. In this **case study methodology**, you might well employ a variety of **methods**. For example, you might want to gather the documents of planning, the documentary evidence and then interview practitioners on how these documents were used. You might want to discuss the issue of 'in-the-moment planning' and how that impacts their ability to plan ahead. You might even want to refine the initial study question to '**How does in the moment planning impact our ability to deliver the EYFS?**' As you start thinking about your project, you will be able to become clearer about the following:

- What you want to find out and why (your topic and rationale for choosing it).
- How you will find out (your methodology and methods).
- The implications that you need to consider (time frame and ethical considerations).
- The worthwhileness of the study (who will benefit? How will you disseminate what you find out to others?).

These are of course just a few possibilities from the initial interest and early years policy. The following section offers broad interest areas you might want to consider when deciding upon your project.

Some further suggestions for early years studies projects

Although policy in some ways always impacts issues that we might discuss in the early years, there are many other worthwhile and interesting areas to explore. Here is a list of some areas of practice that students have chosen to investigate. You might want to note down any that appeal to you as you read through the list.

Play

The benefits of structured and unstructured play

Role play

Rough and tumble play

Freeflow play environments

Gender and play choices

Outdoor play and Forest School approaches

Risky play

Development

Physical development

Language development

Cognitive development

Schemas and development

Social and Moral development

Whether ages and stages matter

Professionalism

The upskilling agenda

What professionalism means

Debating the caring persona attributed to early years practitioners

How early years practitioners see their identity

Stress and the early years practitioner

Interprofessional working

Safeguarding

Working with families

Social conditions

Childcare and affordability issues

Poverty and childhood

Justice and equity in early years provision/practice

Community childcare provision

Welfare

Flourishing children

Mental health promotion

Food and obesity issues

Provision of healthcare

The list of possible topics could go on and on; for example, leadership and management of settings, curriculum, etc. All offer opportunities to question, find out and move forward in practice. Nind, Curtin and Hall (2016) suggest that early years practitioners might want to research pedagogical approaches to practice. They propose that the topic can be thought of in terms of overview, comparison and causation. See if this helps you determine a draft research question.

So how do you decide on an area of study for you?

There are generally three groups of students at this point.

Group 1

There are those who know what they want to research; these students have generally got a pet topic that intrigues them and they have been building up to this opportunity from day one at university. They see this as an opportunity to find out something interesting or to attempt to solve a puzzle that has been worrying them.

Group 2

These students have liked a lot of the content that they have been taught and at least equally have struggled to see the relevance of some ideas. They have an idea of an area that interests them but they are not fully committed and they worry that they will do a lot of work and then change their mind about what they want to do and then find themselves behind their peers.

Group 3

These students haven't a clue about what they want to do. Some admit that they don't really know what they are doing here or how they found themselves in the situation whereby they are thinking about an extended piece of academic work. Sometimes these students have been 'told' to get a degree by their employers, who need a graduate in the workplace. These students can, by the end of the year, become the most passionate about their study as all the balls fall into place, all the ideas connect and then they decide to pursue a master's degree.

It doesn't matter which group you align with because at the end of the day, the starting point is just that the starting point but it is useful to be honest with yourself.

Throughout this book, we will intersperse stories and narratives of students who initially aligned with each of these groups. They are ex-students now who have kindly agreed to share their journeys or reflections of colleagues on their experiences of supporting students.

Moving on

You now have your first choice to make. Are you at this moment in group 1, 2 or 3?

If you are in group 1, you need to ask yourself the following questions: Can I sustain interest in this area of study, which has intrigued me so far, for another year or will I get bored? Have I exhausted the novelty of the learning here for me? If the answer is no, then you are so far along the road already; you know the broad area of your research, and by now you will know some of the key academic writers in the field. You are entitled to feel a little smug at this point.

If you placed yourself in group 1 but are now wondering whether you can sustain your interest for another year, then you either need to look for some novelty in your area of study, something you haven't investigated much yet, or you need to join group 2.

Group 2, look back at the list of possible areas above as well as thinking back over your course content to date and your current experience and work role. Do some further reading around possible topics of interest to see if there is an angle or an issue that motivates you to read further, this might just be your starting point.

Group 3, look through the list of topics and the titles of lectures you have attended and consider which you found most interesting.

Next stage – TASK 1 – you will need a notebook. Look for your group below and complete the task. Group 1 is now being subdivided into

Group 1a – You are the 'Certain I can sustain my interest' group.
Task 1 – Write down five things in your preferred area of study that you want to find out.

Group 1b – 'Not certain my preferred area will continue to interest me' group.
Task 1. Write down five areas that you are interested in, in priority order, with 1 being the most interested and 5 being fairly interested. You will then have some 'fall back on' topics if you need them.

Group 2 – 'Liked the course but couldn't see relevance of it all' group.
Task 1 – Write down the five areas of study that you have found most interesting in your course.

Group 3 – 'Not sure why I am doing this course' group.
Task 1 – Write down five reasons why you are sitting here reading this.

Writing 'because I was told to' is allowed as one. **Link your reasons for being on your course to the topics above or determine what topic from your course it is linked to. Now write a topic list of possible areas for investigation.** For example, one reason for you being on a degree course might be to develop your skills as an educator. What skills are these? Are they pedagogical (about how you educate)? Or linked to specific curriculum areas, e.g., maybe early maths?

Once you have completed this, then move onto Task 2.

All groups – Task 2.

Now you need to find a friend. This friend doesn't necessarily need to be another student but they need to be able to keep asking Why? The friend won't be giving you any answers, they will just make you analyse what you say.

Read your list to a friend, and after each statement on your list, your friend needs to ask why and you need to justify what you have just said as if you were a salesman pitching a product. Have you managed to sell a convincing product

(study)? If so, you are now well on your way to being able to think about your future studies.

When doing this exercise with a group of students, I had a group that was, as they put it, 'stuck in group 3'. When they did this exercise as a group, it became apparent that within 'group 3' there were several students whose motivation for doing the course was necessity. For some, that necessity was to gain a degree in order to keep their current job, and for others, it was a stepping stone to a qualification they needed to have in order to progress their careers. For one, it was simply 'to be better educated', a personal challenge.

The why questions worked to help them decide on a project – here is an example of how it might go:

Q: Why are you here?

A: I was told to come by my employer.

Q: Why?

A: Because we need a graduate in our setting?

Q: Why?

A: Because it is a policy to get a graduate in every setting.

Q: Why?

A: Because they (the government) think you need to be educated to teach young children.

Q: Why?

A: Because they think that it makes for better quality provision.

Q: Why?

The student I was questioning was becoming quite annoyed with my constant whys. This was good because she was showing an emotional response. She felt that she knew her job and did it well but that her professionalism was undervalued. We started to talk about quality agendas and how they can lead to the de-professionalisation of staff. This did interest her, so we at least had something to work with, and since I as a tutor can work with indignation as an emotion, this is great for me. I can feed her material that will develop her emotional response and we will work together to find an issue that excites her. That's what you must do…find your indignation or incredulity and base your study on developing knowledge that allows you to argue against the cause of the indignation. The ability to argue your point of view will give you the confidence to act, to stand your ground and to put forward your reasoned argument. This is the power of education.

At the end of this exercise, you will have started to justify your interests. This is the first step in defining a rationale for your study.

You should now be at the point of having a blunt pencil (raw project). You know the colour of your pencil (the broad area of investigation), and as we go through the book, we will keep sharpening it until it is ready to use.

Getting to a working title

From the start, you need to know that a working title is unlikely to be your final title; your final title will not emerge probably until nearly the end of your study. A working title is just that; it is there to help you shape your project and keep your thinking on track but not to go on autopilot. It will change repeatedly as you learn more and as your thinking develops.

So how does a working title develop?

Task 3

Go back to Task 1 – take one of the areas of interest that raises some emotion in you (excitement, incredulity, anger, etc.).

Now

Write your area of interest as a statement, e.g., I am interested in Child Development.

There you have a working title.

Now add an 'and' or an 'in'.

I am interested in Child Development in literacy.

Or

I am interested in Child Development and learning to read.

Either of these represents starting to get a sharper focus and is a working title, just add research in front and you have.

A Research Project on Child Development and learning to read.

We're there, we have a working title.

A working title signifies the point where you have a project that you could start working on and where that initial work will not be wasted. It will be deepened and sharpened, but not wasted. We are on track once we have a working title.

This brings us to another important point. **Working students lack one major resource, time. You must work smart and work pragmatically.** You cannot waste time as it is such a valuable resource to you. You don't want any reading to be wasted, or any ideas lost. Therefore, you should keep a notebook. You need to be able to revisit bits of your journey that didn't seem significant at the time but that later will become pivotal for further developing your ideas. There are so many times where I have had a great idea, a crystal-clear idea that was simple and had clarity, but I rejected it and then, once enveloped in deeper reading, could no longer see the wood for the trees. This is when you need to go back to your notes to see how you got to where you are now. Thinking and developing ideas is like a loop; you need to be able to go backwards around the loop sometimes to help you move forward. Don't lose your thinking.

Once you have your working title, you need to start organising your reading. You can start this by making a reading/investigation plan, and mind mapping is a great way to start.

Mind mapping

One of the key ways to organise your initial search for sources is to develop a mind or concept map. The mind map should lead you to the key words that you will enter into your library search engines to find the literature that you will need to support your work.

You should keep your work, as you can add ideas to it as you go along.

Mind maps can be constructed using online software or manually with pen and paper; one is as effective as the other, and it is a matter of personal choice.

Mind map software can be found at https://www.edrawsoft.com/.

There is a free version, which is entirely adequate for this task, but the saved work has a watermark.

There are many other free mind map software tools. For some, an app on a phone might be a good suggestion as then you can note down ideas as they come to you.

Suitable apps are

BigHairyGoal

SimpleMind

Mindly

The one you choose is down to personal preference. All offer in-app purchases, so be careful.

My own personal favourite is 'Mindly' because it offers the facility to take photographs and I found this useful as, whilst browsing in the library, I could add photos of the books that I had found as a way of quickly starting to build up a reading list.

If you choose to create a hand-drawn mind map, then choose a large piece of paper. I generally, in sessions, give students an A2 piece of flipchart paper. They put their initial idea/area of interest in the centre and then draw lines to the concepts that link. This document becomes a constant point of reference and we add post-it notes over the top once the paper is full or to layer the concepts.

Another recent and useful too is artificial intelligence (AI) software.

AI software

There has been an increasing number of AI tools that can be of great help to researchers. One of the seemingly most useful is ChatGPT. You must sign up for a free account at ChatGTP and then you are invited to ask a question. The AI software then searches databases to find information to answer your question. The answer is provided in free text, which can then be used by the researcher to follow the leads it provides.

Here is an example of the results of a query asking the software.

Which theorists write about neo-liberalism in early years education?

The response received was:

Several theorists have written about neo-liberalism in early years education, including:

- Margaret Archer, a British sociologist, who has written extensively on the impact of neo-liberal policies on education and has argued that neo-liberalism leads to increased inequality and a narrowing of the curriculum.
- David Harvey, an American geographer and social theorist, who has written about the impact of neo-liberalism on urban spaces and has also discussed the ways in which neo-liberalism has affected education.
- Andreas Fejes, a Swedish sociologist, who has written about the impact of neo-liberal policies on education in Sweden and has argued that these policies have led to increased inequality and a narrowing of the curriculum.
- Susan Robertson, a British sociologist and educational researcher, who has written about the impact of neo-liberal policies on early years education and has argued that these policies have led to a focus on individual achievement and competition, rather than collective well-being.
- Pasi Sahlberg, a Finnish educator and researcher, who has written about the Finnish education system and its contrast with the neo-liberal policies being implemented in many other countries.

(ChatGPT 2023)

Again, this is a tool to help you identify aspects of practice that you might be interested in and to also help you find the names of key theorists who might have contributed to our existing knowledge in that area. There is some controversy in the academic community now about introducing students to this tool. As a team, we view the tool as akin to a word calculator in that the responses you get are only as valuable as the search terms you put in. The answers from the tool are generally quite formulaic and sometimes there are inaccuracies; therefore, it is a tool that is to be used cautiously but is great if you are stuck for ideas as to where to go next.

The next task will encourage you to further explore where your interests might lie.

Task 4

Create a mind map for your working title. At this stage, it can be very simple as in the illustration above.

You can also try some AI questions to help you expand your horizons.

If you are resistant to the use of technology, make yourself explore at least one online mind map application and one app. I was so resistant to this but then quickly saw how this could have saved me so much time in the past. I am now a convert to 'Mindly' and 'ChatGTP'.

Make sure that you store your mind map somewhere as it will become invaluable later in your research journey. Update your mind map with new ideas when they come to you. Look for connections between ideas. The mapping/mind mapping notes and tasks can all be annotated as you go along and keeping track of your thinking will help you when it comes to writing up your project.

The rationale

The rationale is an important part of your project and you will need to be able to communicate this to your supervisor and include it in your final write-up.

The rationale justifies your chosen project. It communicates why the topic is important to you, where you personally stand/position yourself in relation to the topic and how you might have certain experiences or biases that could impact the research. For example, several students each year are often interested in the approaches to certain additional needs because they have personal experience with them; for example, one student was interested in how sign language was used in mainstream reception classes because she had a daughter who was deaf and she didn't feel that the school was adequately prepared to teach deaf children. It is important to understand and communicate the reasons for the research honestly so that readers can then make their own judgements about any bias there might be on the researcher's part.

Here is an example rationale for the above scenario

I intend to investigate how teachers are trained to help deaf children access the curriculum. I myself have a deaf daughter and my experience is that, although she has been allocated a mainstream school place, the school has had no support in preparing for her admission to the school. I intend to interview teachers in mainstream schools to determine how prepared they feel they would be should they have a deaf child in their class. I want to find out whether any preparation is provided to trainee teachers and how successful this is.

Here the student is clearly setting out their position in relation to the research topic and you can tell that the student believes that there is little preparation for the pupil, thereby allowing the reader to appreciate that the starting point of the research might have an element of bias.

Task 5

Think about your topic and your position in relation to it.

Draw a picture of yourself and think about all the things that influence you. This might include your partner, children, work role, family, friends and locality. Do these people/circumstances have any influence over how you view yourself or the topic of your research. After you have thought this through, try to write a draft rationale for your study.

Once you have completed all the tasks in this chapter, you are probably ready to start the next part of the journey, which is working through the ideas with your supervisor.

References

Nind, M., Curtin, A., & Hall, K. (2016). *Research Methods for Pedagogy* (3rd ed.). Bloomsbury Academic.

OpenAI. (2023). *ChatGPT* (Mar 14 version) [Large language model]. https://chat.openai.com/chat

Savin-Baden, M., & Tombs, G. (2017). *Research Methods for Education in the Digital Age* (3rd ed.). Bloomsbury.

Working with your supervisor

Miles Smith

Introduction

Undertaking a complex and extended honours project or dissertation can be daunting to many students, and there can be many challenges throughout the process. However, good research is not carried out in isolation, and throughout your honours-level research, you will receive ongoing support from a supervisor. Collaborating with your supervisor to ensure that the supervision process is effective can result in many benefits; indeed, in addition to the development of skills that are useful for work, and gaining your degree qualification, good supervision can enable you to develop your sense of self-worth and grow your personal and academic identity (Wisker, 2012).

It is important to reflect on the holistic nature of supervision, which, given its protracted timeframe, is much more than a series of tutorials across the year. It is, therefore, worth considering some of the theory that underpins practice in this area. From a range of backgrounds, supervisors will be heavily influenced by their own academic context and professional history, yet it is likely that they will approach supervision with some well-established academic strategies and approaches.

Lee (2012) posits five possible broad approaches to research supervision:

- functional,
- enculturation,
- critical thinking,
- emancipation, and
- relationship development.

However, she notes that practitioners in HE commonly aim to foster students' curiosity and encourage their inquiry-based research skills (Lee, 2012); they are therefore likely to adopt a coaching approach that helps you learn instead of just teaching you (Whitmore, 2002, cited in Lochtie et al., 2018).

This syncs well with the desire for students to become more autonomous, and as mentioned in Chapter 1, this project represents a shift in that autonomy (Anderson, 2005). You now have a chance to generate knowledge that is functionally important, not simply declarative (Biggs, 2003), and, importantly, develop your critical thinking skills.

Critical thinking

Situated within the intellectualism of the secular Western tradition, critical thinking puts dialogic thinking at the forefront of the supervisory process (Lee, 2012). However, thinking – and the processes to foster and develop this – does not need to be aggressively dialectic; rather, the method can be gently Socratic, as in the why questions in Chapter 1. This allows for the generation of new, cooperatively constructed, provisional knowledge. Thus, in order to develop your critical thinking, supervisors will pose challenging questions, linked to the Socratic method of learning, whereby the teacher/tutor keeps delving deeper with repeated extension questions, to prompt you to engage critically and reflectively.

It is not my position here to argue that any particular approach is the most effective; rather, in this chapter, it is my aim to outline some fundamental principles that can be generally followed by students that will help make the supervision work. More specifically, we will explore the relationship between you and your supervisor, what you can expect in terms of support and what to do if the relationship should break down. This is not a one-size-fits-all system, but it should provide you with some clear advice about how to conduct this important relationship and how to ensure that it is successful.

Jess's story

Here is a short commentary from Jess, who completed her dissertation in 2019, in relation to the benefits of the student–supervisor relationship. I have added the italics here:

> For me, my dissertation tutor played a big role in terms of *helping me to feel assured I was going in the right direction with my work.* One of the biggest factors that effected [sic] my confidence and determined how I viewed my tutor was from the amount of knowledge I perceived them to have. For instance, during meetings they could recall various theorists that would be useful and how their ideas could be embedded into the data. Hence, this suggested to me that had a breadth of knowledge and experience behind them, and *it was clear they have helped many others through this laborious process before.*
>
> ...*I was not spoon-fed, rather, given options to explore wider avenues* for my research and this was through my supervisors [sic] expert knowledge as they were able to recall a range of past readings relating to my topic and *it*

was then up to me to explore these and interpret them in accordance with my ideals and understandings.

Reassurance for Jess that she was on track, coupled with an implicit sense that the supervisor was knowledgeable about both her subject and the research process, was crucial to her support. However, Jess' words in the second paragraph are also revealing: Jess needed to take ownership of her own learning, responding to advice about reading, making decisions about what lines of enquiry to pursue and – crucially – reflecting on her own perspectives.

As indicated earlier, there are various approaches to research supervision; however, Jess' clear articulation of a student–supervisor relationship that is centred on scaffolded support, encouragement and the development of the student's knowledge, understanding and skills is arguably at the heart of all good supervision.

Task 1: reflection

Consider the comments in this introductory section. Reflect on the following questions and discuss these openly with someone.

How do you envisage the student–supervisor relationship will work for you?

Does Jess' experience typify what you might expect?

How confident do you feel about taking ideas on board and researching these further?

Do you recognise questioning as a key aspect of learning?

Are you open and reflective about the advice from others?

First meeting with supervisor

At the beginning of the academic year, you will be assigned a supervisor who will oversee your research. The first meeting is integral to getting the process underway, and so it is good to go into this with a clear sense of what you should aim to achieve from this meeting. Be proactive in contacting your supervisor to arrange a meeting; the sooner you get things started, the better, as you will want to get the most out of the experience and make the most of the support offered to you. Take your research notebook along with you. Explain your position in regards to why you intend on researching your specific chosen area. This is where you can try out your rationale.

In this meeting, there are four key aims:

Get to know each other – this is an opportunity to ask each other questions about their backgrounds and experiences. In many cases, you are assigned a supervisor whose interest or research area aligns with your own, and so this is a good time to find out how your supervisor's experience is relevant. It is also useful to indicate in an open and honest way how you feel about carrying out your research, whether you feel daunted by it, confident and keen to get started or somewhere in between. Supervisors are likely to have experience supporting all types of students and projects but will want to know how to tailor their support to suit you as an individual. Bear in mind that whilst this is not a *personal* meeting (and it is therefore important to retain a professional dialogue), an honest and frank approach from the outset will help ensure a personalised approach that leads to consistent progress throughout.

Discuss what you hope to achieve with your research – this is a crucial part of the meeting and should form the core part of the discussion. It is more than likely that at this stage, you already have a good idea of the area of study, but your supervisor may not, and therefore be prepared to talk about your area of interest, the research question, the methodological approach you would like to take as well as any practical matters such as the research site or participants. Your supervisor will inevitably want to know why this research interests you, so be prepared to discuss why the subject matters to you and what you hope to learn from it. Prior to your meeting, either you or your supervisor may suggest sending through a research proposal (if you already have one) so that your supervisor is familiar with your topic ahead of this meeting. At the very least, take along a brainstorm or concept map of the ideas that interest you.

The emergence of a plan – this is crucial from the earliest stages, and following your first meeting, you should be able to begin your project in earnest. The broad and general discussion about your research will ultimately lead to the question of *what happens next*. With your supervisor, and in line with the guidance offered by your institution, you will be able to establish some short-term goals; these may involve the preparation of certain documents (i.e. an application for your project's ethical approval, or you may need to work up a research proposal if you have not already done so), or perhaps some further reading that your supervisor recommends. Whatever these goals are, it is essential that you record them and set a realistic and attainable timeframe by which you hope to complete them. Throughout your project, it is essential that you identify and work to deadlines; discussing what's realistic – but also essential – with your supervisor will keep you on track.

Set a date for your next meeting/contact – the academic year can pass quite rapidly, and there can be a multitude of projects to undertake, of which your honours project/dissertation is but one. So, either before the end of your meeting or arranged by email shortly after, set a date for your next meeting/contact. Note that a meeting is face-to-face, whereas a contact may be an electronic communication; in the early stages, as you prepare key documentation, it may well be that it is better to have contact via email, with your supervisor supporting you with proofreading key documents or early drafts. What is essential from the first meeting is that you know what the subsequent steps are, when these will happen and what you intend to do when you next meet with or contact your supervisor.

Please see Form 1, which will help you prepare for, and record information during, your first meeting.

Task 2: anticipating

Take a look at Form 1 and respond to the following questions:

Can you see how you would make use of this before and during your first meeting?

If you are preparing a project now, what sections could you already complete?

What would you need to do more work for?

Expectations and responsibilities on both sides

From the outset of your research project, it is essential that you have a clear sense of what you can and cannot expect of your supervisor, and what both your and their responsibilities should be. Your institutional framework or documentation will support this, and you should aim to consult it before your first meeting. Knowing what the institutional parameters are for supervision will guide you in terms of your expectations, and it is essential to the success of the supervision that these are adhered to as closely as possible. In particular, the supervision framework will provide guidance for the number of hours supervisors are allocated to support each student, including time for meetings, email correspondence, reading and responding to drafts and marking. Whilst most academics are not clock-watchers, it is important to bear in mind that this can be considerable work, and that in many cases, the time supervisors are deployed for is somewhat on the inadequate side.

However, supervisors take their responsibilities seriously, and – although this cannot be expected on your part – will often go above and beyond in supporting you through the challenges of the research project. Table 2.1 summarises responsibilities for both you and your supervisor in relation to communication, organisation and learning and will help you both moderate your expectations of your supervisor and ensure that they are realistic.

There are a couple of additional points to keep in mind. First, not all academics work full-time, and so it is imperative that you maintain an organised approach if your supervisor is only available on certain days or times. You should also be aware that supervision by a part-time academic may mean a difference in response time to emails; this is something you should seek to clarify early on so you know where you stand and what you can expect. Whilst this may appear to be a negative consideration vis-a-vis academics who are full-time, you must remember that programme or module leaders will do their best to pair you with a supervisor who is going to give you the very best support and has a good knowledge of your area of interest, and this may well be a part-time academic.

Table 2.1 Responsibilities during supervision

	Your responsibilities	**Your supervisor's responsibilities**
Communication	To initiate a first meeting with your supervisor, sending through information as requested	To be available for an initial meeting, setting aside sufficient time to discuss the project
	To email your supervisor in a timely way so there is sufficient time for them to respond to questions or requests	To respond to email contact within the institutional framework (this is often within three working days)
	To request meetings via email (via Outlook or other appropriate institutional diary), booking these in with clear sense of what you intend to do (see Meeting Organiser, Form 2); any cancellations to be made as early as possible	To be available for meetings as requested (in line with the time commitment of their institutional framework), cancelling with as much notice as possible
	To indicate alternative need for communication as necessary, making appropriate request (via diary as appropriate)	To contact student via alternative means (i.e. via telephone/online meeting) if requested (within allocated time framework)
Organisation	To develop clear plans for project and to maintain these in an organised way, ensuring that key project deadlines are met	To support with questions and discussions related to the planning of the project, and suggesting a timeframe (if required)
	To make appropriate back-ups of all work, using cloud storage if viable	Nor your supervisor's responsibility (although they may recommend this)
	To ensure key research documents are produced in a timely way, in line with institutional guidance	To offer feedback on key research documents, suggesting changes as appropriate
	To submit draft work to supervisor at key points, in line with institutional or programme guidance	To offer feedback on written work, in particular with regard to 'academic' content
	To proofread draft work thoroughly, checking grammar, punctuation and spelling (other resources/support may also be available)	To offer some general advice in this area, but not full word-by-word scrutiny or edit of text

(Continued)

Table 2.1 Responsibilities during supervision *(Continued)*

	Your responsibilities	Your supervisor's responsibilities
Learning	To read and make notes about the study in an independent and organised way	To offer suggestions for reading and respond to questions about subject
	To communicate with the research site, initiating contact with gatekeeper and ensuring relevant paperwork is provided as requested (having been seen by supervisor already)	Not your supervisor's responsibility, although they may offer some support if feasible
	To undertake research, collecting and storing data in line with ethical guidance	Not your supervisor's responsibility
	To process data in order to extract key themes and points to present through results and in discussion	To provide support in relation to data analysis, making suggestions for coding and organising (see Chapter 7)
	To complete writing and publication of final project/dissertation in line with institutional guidance	To offer support and feedback on written chapters, and to collaborate on marking of project

On the other hand, due to the wide-ranging interests of students, it is also feasible that you choose an area of research for which there is no specialist at your university. In this instance, the supervisor you are assigned will strive to find out what you know in detail so that they can offer different perspectives and suggest theoretical frameworks or readings to examine that might shed new light on your investigation. Do remember that academics cannot know everything about all subjects. They are though generally very adept at learning, sourcing and synthesising information, understanding critical and analytical perspectives and arguments and cross-fertilising research domains with ideas from other areas or disciplines. Bearing this in mind, do not be anxious if your supervisor is not an expert in a specific niche in the field of study (this is likely to be a bonus, in fact), but do rest assured that they will offer you skilled and expert advice and input and have broad and relatable knowledge and understanding.

Here are Jess' words again about the influence that supervisors (among other educationalists) can have on supporting the development of learners:

Jess's experience

Perhaps not just within higher education, but my whole schooling experience, those who I have felt have a real passion to help me to achieve my goals remain part of my life today as I am training to enter the world of education for my future career, and often, I reflect upon the things they did for me, the interactions they engaged in and the action they took to support me. Their actions and words really have influences me in ways they are likely to be unaware of [...and...] I have taken things from the experience and embedded it into my own practices, or, used the experience to decide what not to do in my practices.

Spend some time now thinking about the implications of:

Task 3: self-awareness

Consider the responsibilities outlined for you and your supervisor in Table 2.1 and respond to the following questions:

How closely does the role outlined align with what you anticipate?

Is there anything here that shocks or surprises you?

What do you perceive to be your strengths in terms of communication, organisation and learning?

How to get the most out of supervision

Integral to the success of your supervision is taking your responsibilities seriously. These are enumerated in Table 2.1; however, here is some more general advice that will help you to make the most of your supervision.

Be proactive

The success and outcomes of your project will largely be determined by how proactive and engaged you are as a researcher and as a student. Make good use of your time and ensure that you make effective use of it. You need to engage independently in your dissertation or project, which will require you to commit time and energy to reading, planning, note-taking, writing, preparing for meetings, carrying out primary research, processing and analysing data, editing, proofreading, developing knowledge and skills in other areas (for instance, your digital knowledge) and disseminating your research. This is a complex range of activities, and to be successful with all of them, you must be proactive from the outset.

Engage in discussion

As discussed earlier, your supervisor will support you with questioning and challenge as they provoke you to reflect on and critically consider the perspectives, approaches and strategies you take in your project. Aim to be involved in these discussions, respond fully and openly to questions and embrace the opportunity to talk about the issues in your work and to ask questions of your own. Discussions with your supervisor and also with peers, practitioners, friends and family and other academics will help drive your project forward, keep you motivated and lead to interesting or novel perspectives and ideas for your work.

Reflect

Reflection can of course happen during or as a result of discussion, but it is also important to take time to think things through independently. To do so, you may wish to keep reflective notes, which can be read and re-read as a way of enhancing your reflections, or you may choose to go for a quiet walk or listen to music as you think your project ideas through. What is most important is that you devote time and create space to reflect at all stages of the project. Try to reflect critically and think through the possible outcomes of your actions.

Read, read and read some more

As you will no doubt be aware, reading in HE can involve engaging with a range of academic texts, from book chapters to papers in journals, and there is also grey literature (i.e., policy documentation) to engage with as well. This may seem obvious, but reading for a large project is complex, and it is important that you develop a disciplined reading habit from the outset of your project. What you read initially may be quite broad, and may feel disjointed, but over time, with the support of your supervisor directing you and challenging you to be more specific, you will begin to hone the scope of your literature search. Be prepared also to encounter texts with complex ideas that you are unfamiliar with; these can be brought to your supervisors for discussion, but do remember also that there is great value in re-reading and that over time your knowledge and understanding will grow, thus enabling you to perceive ideas more clearly. See Chapter 5 on Literature Reviews for more specific advice.

Make notes and record meetings

Linked to the point above, good notetaking (which identifies key aspects or threads from a text, key quotes and ideas, or summarises arguments and points made in supervision discussions) is crucial to your ongoing work on the project. Notes are a repository of information and are indispensable during academic research. Make notes and have these on hand for your supervision meetings, and be prepared to record notes during your meetings. Some supervisors will allow you to digitally record supervisions, so you can use the recordings to go back and make further notes, but it is also good to write as you discuss. Your supervisor will encourage this and give you time to jot down key points – keep them clear in a notebook and make sure you follow up on any points discussed. Make sure that you store references to useful texts in a bibliography so that you do not have to go searching for them later. It is especially important to keep a note of page numbers for direct citations that you have noted.

Have an open mind

Critical to the success of any project and collaboration is having an open mind, being prepared to listen to others and not assuming that we are in a position of greater knowledge or authority. Whilst you may not agree with everything your supervisor says, do have an open mind and listen carefully to the ideas put forward. Equally, be open to the idea of changing how you think; good supervision and good research can be incredibly transformational and have the potential to influence your future professional and academic choices. Being open-minded through the process, therefore, can lead to greater insight and can empower your decision-making.

Meet deadlines

Throughout your project/dissertation year, there will be one deadline that sticks in your mind: that of your final submission. However, there will be other deadlines along the way, which could include your application for ethical approval from your institution, as well as formative submissions. Recognising the broad nature of the project, though, will help you identify other deadlines and dates to work to, such as contacting gatekeepers if you are undertaking primary research, or processing and analysing data. All stages of a project will take time, so discuss the various stages with your supervisor and map out the year so you understand what you need to do and by when.

Respond to/act on feedback

Your supervisor will want to see that you are responding throughout the project to their feedback and challenges. This will come through in your written work, but also in the development of the project. It is, of course, your work, and you should make the decisions, but there is real value in using your supervisor's ideas to push at the boundaries of your knowledge and understanding.

To support you further with your supervision, Form 2 has been developed for use in supervision meetings. Have a look at this and complete the following task.

Task 4: Meeting organiser

Familiarise yourself with Form 2 (Meeting Organiser).

This is structured to be flexible and adaptable for any meeting with your supervisor. You should know what you want to discuss, and you should have any relevant information with you. Use of a form like this will enable you to make the best use of your time with your supervisor while also showing that you are engaging in a responsible and organised way.

Have you used a form like this before?

How much time do you think you will need to prepare for a meeting?

Where do you plan to keep your working notes for the project?

Dealing with issues in your supervision

It is possible that issues may arise in your supervision; indeed, it is noted in the literature that problems may occur with the research, the project/dissertation writing and – potentially – with the supervision itself. Wisker (2012) identifies a number of generic issues: some are practical or logistical (time management, actualisation of the project through to completion), others are learning-centered (problem-solving, conceptualisation and critical thinking) and some relate to modes of expression (writing for an audience and articulation). Wisker (2012) suggests that many students are not naturally inclined to in-depth study of this nature and may struggle as they navigate uncertainty towards the acquisition of threshold concepts (moments of learning marked by insight and order); furthermore, given the relatively free choice students can have for this assessment, supervisors may find themselves in unknown territory in terms of subject knowledge.

Whatever the issues (see Table 2.2), there are strategies you can take to help improve matters, and relations – if they have deteriorated for some reason – can be nurtured back to good health. Please note that your institution will have procedures in place to support this as well, so this advice should be read in tandem with any institutional guidance. The following are four of the most common issues and (tiered) responses:

Table 2.2 Issues with supervision

Issue	Your response
Your supervisor is not communicating with you in a timely way	This should be in line with the institutional guidelines, but you should also check whether your supervisor is part-time as this may impact when they are able to engage Ask your supervisor to clarify when they will respond to you; this can be done in a meeting, or in a polite request via email If the supervisor does not respond at all, reach out to another member of the academic team, or the module or course lead, who will be able to follow this up

(Continued)

Table 2.2 Issues with supervision *(Continued)*

Issue	Your response
Your supervisor is recommending that you take a different approach and you are not comfortable with this	Make sure you have reflected critically and openly on the advice that your supervisor has given; refer back to your notes and consider the purpose and nature of the advice Speak to/contact your supervisor and ask them to clarify any recommendations made previously if you are unsure about these Present an alternative case to your supervisor; it is good to justify and rationalise the decisions we make, and this may well fed into a written component of your project
Your supervisor has not given you useful feedback on your work	Review the feedback and check through the various points raised; have you responded to these and considered all of them fully? Speak to/contact your supervisor and pose any additional questions that you may have; be specific when you do this, asking more than 'Is this good?' You may wish to ask if the argument is well-constructed, or if the texts used to support the discussion are appropriate, or if you have been critical enough in your analysis If you feel the advice is not useful at all, speak to/contact the module or course lead
You don't get on with your supervisor	It is great if the relationship between supervisor and student is a friendly one, but this cannot be an expectation; what is important is that the relationship is respectful and professional; have you reflected on this? Be mindful about comparing your supervisor with your friend's supervisor, especially in the early stages of a project; working with your supervisor over time will help your relationship grow, so aim to invest time in this Plan your first and subsequent meetings and see how the relationship develops Have an open mind – in your professional life, you will encounter all sorts of people, so it is a good opportunity for personal and professional growth to work with someone who you do not feel really positive about As a last resort, talk to your module or course lead

Conclusion

There are huge advantages to working closely with an academic on your dissertation/project, and you can reap many rewards from the experience if you engage positively and proactively. In many ways, supervision exemplifies the apex of learning in the Western tradition, and certainly within higher education, it can lead to excellent outcomes for students: a heightened sense of self-worth, greater self-efficacy and development of a range of soft and power skills for academic or professional work. Your supervisor is an integral part of this, but it is up to you to dedicate yourself to this process and take the control needed for success.

References

Anderson, C. (2005). Enabling and Shaping Understanding through Tutorials. *The Experience of Learning Implications for Teaching and Studying in Higher Education. 3rd (Internet) Edition*, (52), 184–197. https://doi.org/10.1080/03055690701423069

Biggs, J. (2003). *Aligning Teaching and Constructing Learning: Applying Constructivism and SOLO Taxonomy in Higher Education*. The Society for Research into Higher Education & Open University Press.

Lee, A. (2012). *Successful Research Supervision: Advising Students Doing Research*. Abingdon: Routledge.

Lochtie, D., McIntosh, E., Stork, A., & Walker, B. (2018). *Effective Personal Tutoring in Higher Education* (3rd ed.). Critical Publishing.

Wisker, G. (2012). *The Good Supervisor* (2nd ed.). Palgrave Macmillan.

3 Methodology and methods
Selina Day

In the previous chapter, Miles explored the supervision process. Knowing the area that you wish to explore is obviously important but then the next question is how will I start to find answers to my research questions? This is where we turn to methodology and methods.

If you think of methodology as a toolbox and the methods as tools (an analogy I return to later), then you will be well prepared for this chapter.

Methodology (the toolbox) refers to the design of the study, the selection of participants, the data collection methods, how these are analysed and how they are presented. The methodology is the whole logical process of the research, the box that contains everything and they (the tools) must fit in the toolbox completely.

Methods are the tools that you use from the toolbox.

Supervisors and practicalities of choosing a methodology and the methods

When I first met my project supervisors, the first area they wanted to discuss was their methods for data collection. For many, it can be a daunting task to consider, whilst for others it is an exciting proposition, but for everyone, it is a question that will take much consideration. We will start by looking at the important questions you need to ask yourself and discuss with your supervisor. We will then look at the different methods for data collection, what sort of data each method can gather and evaluate the pros and cons for each. Throughout this chapter, I will provide hypothetical examples of the ethical considerations that you will need to be aware of before, during and after the data collection process. Make sure that you do not attempt to collect any data until you have ethical clearance. This is discussed in Chapters 4 and 6.

What sort of data will help me answer my research question(s)?

Is my methodology predominantly reliant on qualitative responses or quantitative ones?

Quantitative or qualitative ... that is the question.

In your lectures or discussions with supervisors, you would have heard of the terms quantitative or qualitative methods. The qualitative versus quantitative debate has been extensively discussed, with some researchers arguing that quantitative is better than qualitative. Before we can discuss why this is not necessarily the case, a good starting point for your investigation of research methods is to understand what we mean by these two terms, how they might link back to your philosophical belief around knowledge (your epistemological position) and how they might be useful to your research.

An example

Have you ever been stopped in a shopping mall and been asked the question 'Can I have a moment of your time?' You are then asked to fill out a questionnaire about which shops you have entered and on a scale of 1–10 how you have enjoyed your shopping experience? If so, then you have participated in quantitative research. The aim of quantitative research is to gather a large set of data within short amount of time. This scaling of the answers numerically reduces significantly the time needed for the participant to answer wordy questions. This large amount of data can then be 'measured and represented by numbers' (Koshy, 2009, p. 79). This can be from gathering many questionnaire responses or a vast amount of test results. Due to the large amount of data received, it is often necessary to analyse the data with a statistical approach where it will be presented using tables, charts and graphs. This approach is sometimes called scientific method as all the parameters are controlled; no rogue answers are collected (although you might have a spoilt questionnaire if the instructions haven't been followed).

Whilst quantitative data generate statistics and numbers, qualitative data explore experiences, attitudes and individual views. The purpose of qualitative data is to gain an in-depth understanding of a topic or issue and, as such, it is often the main choice of social science researchers such as yourselves as you are often looking at questions that are about complex professional practices or situations. Due to the complex nature of the responses, few people are needed to gain rich data. The time taken to gain responses from the participants and to analyse the individualistic nature of responses can be extensive.

Prior to our first meeting, I ask my students to consider Dawson's (2019, p.10) 'five Ws':

- *What* is my research?
- *Why* do I want to do the research?
- *Who* are my research participants?
- *Where* am I going to do the research?
- *When* am I going to do my research?

One of the misconceptions that students have is that they need to have a variety of different methods for collecting data. Whilst some questions lend themselves to a mixed methodology whereby methods are selected to maximise understanding, some questions lend themselves to a simple method such as a survey, a focus group or a case study. In such cases, using multiple methods may not add any significant value to the research. However, in some cases, using multiple methods can provide a more comprehensive understanding of the phenomenon under investigation.

Imagine that you are trying to fix a leaky tap in your kitchen. You go into your tool bag (your methodology) and you have an array of different tools (your methods) all with different functions. You find a hammer in your toolbox; even though you have potential to use the tool, would you use it to fix your pipe? – I hope the answer is no! Even though you may have a variety of tools at your disposal, you choose the tool that is going to solve the problem and complete the objective.

This is the same when planning which methods you intend to use to gather your data. If you choose lots of different tools, they may not provide data that is relevant to your aims. I often discuss with my students that it is not always the variety of the methods or the amount of data that you obtain, it is the quality of the data that you collect that will support your aims and 'complete your objective'. If you do not pick the correct toolbox (methodology) and the best tools (methods) for the job (research aims), then you may find that you have no depth or no data that will be able to complete your data analysis leading to answering your question.

So, you might determine that the best way of researching your question is either quantitative or qualitative or that you would like to combine the two. This is called mixed method.

Methodology again

You need to be clear on your philosophical beliefs and from the start to the end of your research journey and regularly remind yourself of the task at hand...you need to be able to analyse data to justify your conclusions. You need to know how you see knowledge. This is known as your ontological position.

Ontology is the way we see the world. There are two main ontological positions; the first is realism. Realists believe that knowledge is available independently of the researcher. Realists believe that the truth is independent of the researcher or participants and that findings could be replicated in other situations.

The second main ontological position is constructivism. Constructivists believe that reality is constructed by people. It can be constructed by individuals or groups but is specific to that study. This is why the rationale and explaining your position (Chapter 1) are so important. This allows the readers of your research to understand your reality and how that was influential throughout the project.

The ontological position of the researcher determines the following:

- the choice of methodology and methods;
- the way in which the data is collected and analysed; and
- the way in which the data is interpreted, and conclusions drawn.

Epistemology, another philosophical term, is what you believe constitutes knowledge. Your epistemological position determines whether you judge someone's reflection and analysis of an observed event to be true. You might only consider evidence that is replicated many times in many situations to be true knowledge. If so, your epistemological position is likely to be scientifically orientated. Knowing what you consider to be valid truths will again shape your methodology and methods. In the following section, we will be looking at the different methods you can plan to undertake depending on the data you wish to gather to answer your research questions. We start with the sample population who hold the knowledge you wish to glean.

The sample

Having determined your research area, your questions and the types of methods that fit with your beliefs and purpose, you then need to consider the sample of the population that will help to answer your question. Who will be your research participants? The chapter on ethics will provide further information on this as there might be ethical implications in choosing certain demographic features, e.g., children as research participants. What you do need to consider here is who the population are that you need to research to answer your questions. You need to consider the size and variety within your sample. So, for example, if you are researching the use of the sandpit in the outdoor environment for creative play and you are primarily going to use observation to do this, you need to decide on whether you are going to try to observe all the children who have access to the said sandpit or whether you are going to monitor a selection of children. If a selection and therefore a 'sample', how will you choose them? Boys/Girls? 3 year olds/4 year olds? How many can you realistically observe? How many sessions? and so on. So any one decision then leads to the need to make many more decisions. The methodology is there to help and guide you in making those decisions.

Using questionnaires to gain data

Using questionnaires can be a powerful tool to collect a vast range and amount of data. Some students find that they use questionnaires at the beginning of the data collection process. At this stage, it can provide an understanding of the context of the topic or act as a baseline of the attitudes or feelings of the participants. This can then form the basis of follow-up interviews if a deeper understanding is needed.

Questionnaires

Before planning your questionnaire, there are several points that need to be considered. First, you will need to decide the type of participants/sample you are intending to distribute your questionnaires to? This question is important as it will allow you to identify not only the size and nature of the population group but also the style of the questionnaire. Unlike interviews, most questionnaires will be completed independently without any prompts or support from the researcher. Once you have decided on your intended sample, you will then need to identify what the intentions are for the questionnaire. You will need to consider the **objectives**, **concepts** and **issues** that your questionnaire will cover – linking back to your aims and your literature review will support your understanding and awareness of this.

If you are intending for a 4-year old to complete a questionnaire, then the use of complex language may impact the children's ability to understand the questions and thus lead to inaccurate results. The ability of the child to select an answer independently also needs consideration, and hence the development of picture-based or graphic questionnaires.

With adults, we also need to think about the reading comprehension of the participants when planning the questionnaires. If the participant is not a professional in your field of study, then you may need to give descriptions of terminology. Furthermore, not all questionnaires need to be in the written form.

In one of my first supervisions, a student was working with a group of children where English was not their first language. To overcome the barriers, we discussed the idea of using imagery to show what the question meant. Koshy (2010) and Clark (2017) discuss the use of alternative ways to show feelings or opinions in a response to a question. This could include 'smiley faces' or emojis to show feelings or opinions in response to a question.

You may intend to get a sense of a participant's opinion surrounding a topic or issue. The Likert-style questions are designed to measure opinions and feelings about a topic in a way where it can still be statistically analysed using a scale format (Joshi et al., 2015).

For example, in a study looking at young children's visit to a public library for the first time, it was noted how they were drawn to works by a specific author. In order to establish the practitioners' views on this, the survey questionnaire asked the practitioners to read statements and acknowledge their response at the time. For example, the statement might read

> 'I was surprised by how many children picked up the David Walliams's book first'.

- Strongly agree
- Agree
- Neither disagree or agree

- Disagree

- Strongly disagree

'On a scale of 1–5, how much do you like David Walliams's picture books?'

- 1 – I do not like them at all.

- 2 – I don't like many of his books.

- 3 – I neither like or dislike his books.

- 4 – I like reading his books.

- 5 – I really like his books.

The odd number of possible responses is on a sliding scale of opinion and is designed as such to force the participant to give an opinion rather than being neutral (Wood and Smith, 2016). We must recognise that this may allow for a forced response and therefore has the potential to not give a true representation of a participant's true feelings and thus produce false results.

When constructing your questionnaire, you must also be clear on how you are wanting to analyse the data that you have collected. There are three types of questionnaires that you must be aware of as these will impact the types of questions asked, resulting in different types of responses from the participants, and thus may require a different approach to analysing.

- Closed-ended

- Open-ended

- Combination of both closed and open-ended

Closed-ended questions are often the type of questionnaires that you have encountered when approached in a public place. If we link back to our shopping mall experience, this type of questionnaire was structured where you chose answers that generate statistical data that would allow a for a greater ease of analysis. For example, the question might have been:

Do you shop here often? Yes or No

You may intend to get a sense of a participant's opinion surrounding a topic or issue. The Likert-style questions are designed to measure opinions and feelings about a topic in a way where it can still be statistically analysed with a scale format. Open-ended questionnaires allow a narrative response, so 'Do you shop here often?' could be answered with a qualified answer, e.g., Yes if the weather is fine. A combination questionnaire could ask 'Do you shop here often?' and allow yes or no and then allow a further response to the question 'why?' thus generating richer data and giving some insight into the specific behaviours of the shopper.

So questionnaires are an extremely helpful tool. Think about whether they would be useful in your research project.

Task 1

Answer the following questions:

> Would a questionnaire help me to answer my research question? If yes, then…
>> Who would be the respondents?
>> Do I want closed questions that I can analyse quantitively or open questions that require a narrative response or do I want a mix of the two?
>> What number of questionnaires do I have time to analyse?
>> How do I select who is invited to fill one in? This is your sample.
>> What format should the questionnaire take to get responses from the specific participants (think about how if you are doing research with young children, you could facilitate a response)
>> How would I distribute the questionnaire and how would I get the replies? There is a lot to think about here: paper copies in person, emailed, through social media? A useful book that looks at the use of electronic means is 'Research Methods for Education in the Digital Age' by Savin-Baden and Tombs (2017).

Online tools such as Survey Monkey or Google Forms provide a quick and easy way to gather and analyse a lot of data. Through social media and the instant access to your connections, it has the advantage of reaching a larger population with a larger geographical scope within a short time frame. Whilst this can be appealing, you must be aware of the ethical implications that need to be considered for both the participant and researcher. The potential of anonymity on social media can result in a participant not being identified and thus there are implications for participants being unable to withdraw their consent for the data being part of the research. Furthermore, Brookes et al. (2014, p. 73) highlight the impact that anonymity has on the ability to 'ascertain if participants were able/or allowed to consent for themselves' (e.g. if the survey is intended for participants over the age of 18). Given all the advantages and disadvantages of questionnaire as a tool for research, Nind et al. (2016, pp. 82–83) provide a useful table for determining the usefulness of questionnaires to researchers who are looking specifically at early years practice. They suggest that questionnaires might be useful for (adapted from Nind et al., 2016)

- getting an overview or making comparisons,
- finding out who holds what sort of pedagogical knowledge,
- determining teachers' pedagogic beliefs,

- determining the causation, and
- determining the characteristics of effective early years pedagogies.

In actual research where the children are the research participants, they are less useful.

So questionnaires are undoubtedly one of the tools in the toolkit, but they are often used in conjunction with other methods such as a follow-up interview or observation in a mixed-methods research design.

Interviews

Interviews are another method that is frequently used in research. It is a great way to gather a set of responses that have the potential to be richer and sometimes portray a more honest perspective and insight from participants (Koshy, 2010). Whilst interviews can bring a deeper understanding of a topic or situation, you must carefully plan beforehand how you will structure or organise your interview to elicit rich data.

Like questionnaires, there are three types of interviews:

- Structured interviews
- Semi-structured interviews
- Unstructured interviews

The difference between these types of interviews is dependent on the planning of your interview and the level of predetermined structure you want (Wood and Smith, 2016). Structured interviews have a strong correlation to questionnaires. You plan a set of pre-determined questions that are the only questions that you ask the participant and you do not deviate from these questions. A semi-structured interview prepares not only a set of questions like a structured interview, but they are also to be viewed as starting points to develop and expand the responses from the participants. Based on the participant's answer, you may ask a series of prepared sub-questions to gather more information by probing further. As a result, during the interview, you may ask more than the pre-determined base questions you originally prepared. Finally, there is the option of an unstructured interview, where your interview is focused on your focus area rather than specific questions. This results in a more organically grown interview where questions are shaped and developed through the responses and dialogue of the participant. Whilst easier to compare structured interviews and thus simpler to analyse the data, you will need to recognise that you will be accepting the responses from the participants and probing deeper. In comparison to structured interviews, those that are semi-structured or unstructured allow you to elicit more information or perceptions surrounding your focus area and may supply data that you had not originally planned for. Whilst this can bring some surprise and depth to your data, it can also

> **CASE STUDY: Ryan was a final year degree student and a full-time teaching assistant.**
>
> *Ryan decided to focus his project on his school's outdoor play area and the impact it has on social development. He started his data collection with asking the children in his class (4-5 year olds) to take pictures with a digital camera of the areas they liked to play with their friends. He then printed out these pictures and conducted one-to-one interviews with the children using the images as a stimulus for conversation. Using appropriate language for the children, Ryan asked children where the photos were taken, their thoughts about the photographed area and further asked them to give examples of when they played with friends there and the games that they played. Whilst the child spoke, Ryan would use post-its to write the child's responses and place them around the focal photograph.*

bring challenges when analysing your data and can lead to difficulties in remaining neutral and unbiased.

Interviews can also be conducted with the use of an artefact or images as a tool for a stimulus. 'Stimulated recall interview' is a method that can evoke responses or memories and focus dialogue in relation to the prompt (Wood and Smith, 2016). This method could be used, for example, if a learning or research activity had been conducted previously, and this would stimulate the participants memories of what they did. The following case study shows the potential of using images or artefacts as stimulus for deeper discussion.

So, in this study, Ryan used semi-structured interviews around the photographic artefacts that the children had taken. The children were involved in the research, and Ryan explained to them the purpose of the research, which was to stimulate ideas for the staff team to further develop the outdoor environment. It is often a good idea when interviewing young children to take a semi-structured approach as often their responses can surprise you, and you will by default want to ask a follow-up question simply to clarify the first answer.

Considerations when planning interviews

Before conducting the interview, you must consider the setting up and preparation of the interview ready for when you start the questioning process.

- *Where the interview will be conducted?* Environments for interviews need to feel comfortable for both you and the participant, which allows the participant to feel able to discuss the questions asked.

- *The time taken to conduct the interview.* You will need to plan your interview around a time scale. Interviews should take no longer than 30–45 minutes for adults and 15–20 minutes for a child.

- *How to start the interview?* Introduce yourself and explain the purpose of your interview and how their input will help your research. Make sure you give them the opportunity to give you their consent and the ability to withdraw.

- *Which question will you start with?* Open your questioning with a simple question that does not need the participant to give an opinion or perspective.

- *How will you record the interview?* Interviews have the potential to produce lots of data. The use of a tape or video recorder will allow you to focus on what is being said rather than transcribing key points; however, this may cause participants to be cautious and intimidated.

Once you have conducted the interview, you will then need to write up the interview. If you voice or video recorded the interview, you will need to listen back to the interview and transcribe the whole interview to ensure the accuracy of what was said. Whilst there are some software programmes that allow the process to be quicker (Dragon or Otter, for example), it can still be time-consuming and will need to be considered when planning your honours project. Think about how many interviews you can carry out and analyse in your given time frame. Think about how many participants you need to get a broad sample of the target population.

In Ryan's case, the class consisted of children who were just four and those who were nearly six. Developmentally, there could be a lot of difference in their needs, so your sample needs to consider any diversity that exists in the population (in this case, the class) that is being studied. You need to ask yourself, how do I get a cross section of the class in my 'manageable' sample. All your decision-making needs to be documented in your methodology so that the reader can understand how you selected the sample, this is often called the recruitment method. Do you ask for volunteers (thereby not necessarily getting a cross section of the population being studied) or do you select participants based on certain criteria, e.g., one boy and one girl aged 4–5 and one boy one girl aged 5–6. Whatever you decide to do, you need to document your choice and the rationale behind it. Another useful tool when researching early years environments is observation.

Observations

Have you ever gone into a coffee shop, sat by the window and watched people pass by? At some point in our lives, we would have observed people; this can be intentional or nonintentional. Yet observing people around us is a natural human process and one that has long been used in research and can play an important part in your data collection process. It is often used alongside other types of data to support the triangulation of your research. Triangulation is described by Wood and Smith (2016 p. 99) as 'a process where data from different collection techniques are compared to ascertain if there are common features or themes'. So if we go back to the analogy of the toolkit, we might use more than one tool to finish a job and to make sure that everything is secure.

If you are considering using observations as part of your data collection process, then you must be aware of the two different types of observations and which type will be most appropriate to your research.

- Non-participant observations
- Participant observations

Nonparticipant observation is less intrusive on the participants and involves observing the conditions, actions and behaviours at that moment in time. Often, researchers place themselves in the corner of a room, walking around or standing from afar in an outdoor learning environment. As you only have that moment to capture the data and the environment might have a lot happening, you will need to consider what you are actively looking for during these observations. Before conducting the observation, you will need to ask yourself what your intentions are. Will you be observing the behaviour of children, the types of discussions or language used by the children or teacher or maybe you are looking for the number of times the children use a particular type of equipment? These different types of data will require you to consider structuring your observations through the use of checklists, observation sheets and schedules (Koshy, 2010) so you can focus your observations so that they can provide data that will be useful for your analysis.

Participant observation is used to 'achieve intimate knowledge of the group of people who are subjects for the research' (Matthews & Ross, 2010, p. 257). Participant observation is often employed by researchers who work in educational settings or whose research is focused on classroom implementations or behaviours. It involves the researcher being part of the environment and interacting with the participants, rather than being on the periphery. You will need to take on a dual role, one that of researcher and one of teacher or teaching assistant. This can lead to challenges where Cohen et al. (2017) argue that a researcher has the potential to be too subjective when collecting data, and thus from the start, the researcher will need to acknowledge the potential for bias. You will also need to be aware of how you will collect the data during the observations. Some researchers opt to voice or video record the observation sessions and have an activity plan or grid where annotations can be made.

Like all data collection methods, during the planning stage, you must carefully consider all elements surrounding the observation process. You must consider the following:

- If an outsider to the context you need to ask – How will I introduce myself to the group?

- If the group knows you, how will I discuss my role during the observation? You will need to think about the process of informed consent and anonymity. This can be particularly tricky if the observation is within a setting you are employed at.

- How will I limit my impact on the dynamics of the environment? Children have the potential to act different or want to enquire what you are writing or want your attention. This tends to diminish over time, but you may want to look at research discussing the Hawthorne effect. I find Cohen et al.'s (2017) book 'Research Methods in Education' a good starting point.

- How will I record the data obtained during the observation?

For anyone interested in using observation, the book 'Child Observation for Learning and Research' by Papatheodorou and Luff (2011) is very helpful.

Gathering evidence from documents

Sometimes in early years research, documentary evidence in its various forms is very useful.

Sometimes you may feel that gathering other forms of data might support and give context for your research or show the progress of a child. Furthermore, it may give you some information that may confirm or contradict what has been claimed to be happening in educational practice. Evidence from documents may include the following: pupil's work, setting policies and action plans, minutes from meetings and other published documents. Obviously, there are access and confidentiality issues with some of these documents, and the appropriate gatekeepers need to give permission (see Chapter 4).

Artwork can be a great way to gather children's opinions, feelings and views about a topic. During participant observations, interviews or focus groups, you will ask children to draw, paint or produce artwork that allows an alternative way to voice their responses when the child may be unable to offer other forms of verbal or written communication.

Like artwork, photographs, particularly when conducting research in early years settings, can provide evidence of child engagement in an activity, or on a piece of equipment. As discussed within the interview section, they can form a focus for discussions and have the potential for more in-depth data. Another way to present photographs is to print them and allow children to decide which images they would like in a scrapbook and they can then be annotated through the discussions with the children. Alison Clark's (2017) book *Listening to Young Children* discusses the process of asking children to take photographs and using them to form discussions and to produce displays and scrapbooks. This is often termed pedagogical documentation and can provide rich evidence of a child's lived experience. Clark and Moss's (2005) *Spaces to Play* gives many examples of this.

> **CASE STUDY**
>
> Dana decided to conduct research with migrant children aged between 3 and 6 years. Through focus groups, Dana asked the children to paint their favourite thing about their school in the United Kingdom. Whilst some children remained silent, other children were able to discuss what they were drawing and what it represented. These discussions led to some in-depth emotions and perceptions that were from the stimulus of the drawings. Dana realised that she had gathered rich data and that, through the discussion of the children's artwork, there was no need for interpretation of what their art represented, unlike their words, which needed to pass through an interpreter.

Other creative methods to gather data can be found in Hall and Wall's (2019) *Research Methods for Understanding Professional Learning* published by Bloomsbury. Their 'Tools for Enquiry' chapter includes advice on gathering data using cartoons and comics, mapping environments, diamond ranking and art as well as more traditional tools.

Each tool is clearly explained with exemplars and it is a resource that I direct students to once they have an overall idea of their beliefs about knowledge and an initial area of research interest. For those interested in Pedagogical Documentation and the usefulness in research, I recommend the book *Journeys: reconceptualizing early childhood practices through pedagogical narration* (Pacini-Ketchabaw et al., 2015)

Conclusion

This chapter aimed to give you an introduction and make you aware of questions that may be posed during the design and implementation of the research process. It has been highlighted that whilst this can be an exciting prospect for you, it might be recognised that it takes careful consideration not only of which method may best support your aims but also to consider ethical considerations that each method may bring. In the 'Further reading' section, I have produced a list of books that will support your journey and I would recommend contacting your supervisor who can bring their experience and knowledge to support and critique your ideas. Chapter 6 further explores data collection, and once you have the necessary permissions to start your research, this chapter will act as a useful checklist of decision-making at that point.

Further reading

Cohen, L., Manion, L., & Morrison, K. (2017). *Research Methods in Education*. Routledge.
Papatheodorou, T. and Luff, P. (2011). *Child Observation for Learning and Research*. SAGE.

References

Brooks, R., Riele, K., Maguire, M., & Te Riele, K. (2014). *Ethics and Education Research* (3rd ed.). SAGE Publications.

Clark, A. (2017). *Listening to Young Children: A Guide to Understanding and Using the Mosaic Approach* (3rd ed.). Jessica Kingsley Publishers.

Clark, A., & Moss, P. (2005). *Spaces to Play: More Listening to Young Children Using the Mosaic Approach* (3rd ed.). National Children's Bureau.

Dawson, C. (2019). *Introduction to Research Methods: A Practical Guide for Anyone Undertaking a Research Project* (3rd ed.). Robinson.

Hall, E., & Wall, K. (2019). *Research Methods for Understanding Professional Learning* (1st ed.). Bloomsbury

Joshi, A., Kale, S., Chandel, S., & Pal, D. (2015). Likert Scale: Explored and Explained. *British Journal of Applied Science & Technology*, 7(4), 396–403. https://doi.org/10.9734/bjast/2015/14975

Koshy, V. (2009). *Action Research for Improving Educational Practice*. SAGE.

Koshy, V. (2010). *Action Research for Improving Educational Practice: A Step-by-Step Guide* (2nd ed.). SAGE Publications Ltd.

Matthews, B., & Ross, L. (2010). *Research Methods: A Practical Guide for the Social Sciences* (3rd ed.). Pearson Longman.

Nind, M., Curtin, A., & Hall, K. (2016). *Research Methods for Pedagogy* (3rd ed.). Bloomsbury.

Pacini-Ketchabaw, V., Nxumalo, F., Kocher, L. L. M., Elliot, E., & Sanchez, A. (2015). *Journeys: Reconceptualizing Early Childhood Practices through Pedagogical Narration* (3rd ed.). University of Toronto Press.

Papatheodorou, T., Luff, P., & Gill, J. (2013). *Child Observation for Learning and Research*. Taylor & Francis.

Savin-Baden, M., & Tombs, G. (2017). *Research Methods for Education in the Digital Age* (3rd ed.). Bloomsbury.

Wood, P., & Smith, J. (2016). *Educational Research: Taking the Plunge* (3rd ed.). Independent Thinking Press.

4 Gaining ethical approval
Jonathan Harvey

Ethical considerations in your research

Introduction

This chapter seeks to take you through the ethics process that you will have to complete for your research. We will first cover the reasons for ethics in research and state the pivotal space this occupies within the research process. After this, a simple history of research ethics is given, and some major points in research ethics are discussed. We encourage you to address issues of power within the research process, which gives a sound appreciation of the reasons behind the requirements of ethics panels.

Finally, because of our close consultation with the 2014 guidelines for ethical research provided by the European Early Childhood Education Research Association (EECERA) we discuss documents you may have to produce as part of your research project, such as ethical approval consent forms and information sheets.

Why ethics?

The question of the reason behind ethics approval, or simply put, 'why ethics?' is a truly relevant question and one that is often asked by students. To try and address this question, we will briefly track the history of research ethics with the aim of providing a sound justification for the reasons for such processes. However, rather than viewing the ethical review process as simply another hoop to jump through, it is best viewed as a great opportunity to think through the reasons for your approach to the topic, and therefore can be used to inform your thinking around the whole research project. If the ethics review process is thought of like this, you can capitalise on the thinking and, importantly, the work that you do for the ethics review process and use this in other aspects of your project. Moreover, gaining ethics approval should not be thought of as an isolated process; rather, it is one that occurs throughout the planning phase of the research. It is part of your methodology as you will be carefully considering the place of the research participants and what you will do with the data that they 'gift' you.

Task 1

What are your initial thoughts about what may be the major ethical complexities of your research?

How did ethics become a key part of the research process?

There are some important moments in the history of research ethics, and it is a good idea to be familiar with these moments in order to gain a sophisticated understanding of the ethics approval process.

Nuremberg Code 1948

A pivotal document in the development of research ethics was the 'Nuremberg code', which was established in 1948 and declared that 'research subjects [participants] should give consent and that the benefits of the research must outweigh the risks'. This document came about in direct response to the actions of 23 German physicians and administrators who carried out medical experiments on prisoners without gaining their consent as part of the Nazi Germany regime. Most of the participants died or were severely disabled as a result. Although not enforceable by law, the Nuremberg Code was the first document that referred to the need for voluntary participation and informed consent in research.

Declaration of Helsinki 1964

In 1964, the Declaration of Helsinki represented the issue of research ethics being taken more seriously. The declaration has been updated four times since and establishes some firm rules for good practice in research. The main components include:

- Informed consent should at all times be gained.
- The risks of the research should not outweigh the benefits.
- All research needs to be approved by a committee before it starts.

Key points in this section:

'Nuremberg code' (1948) research subjects [participants] should give consent and that the benefits of the research must outweigh the risks.

Declaration of Helsinki (1964) is the first establishment of guidelines for the ethical complexities of research.

How does this relate to my research?

The basic premise of research ethics is that research should not do any harm to participants. As we have seen, the recognition of the need for research to be ethical came from medical research. However, this is not to say that the same ethical principles of research do not apply to educational research. An idea that is repeated many times during this chapter is that thinking through the ethical complexities of research gives the researcher time to think about many important aspects of the research process. For example, as is common for educational research, it may be decided that the research needs to have some intended benefit for the participants. The ethics process is an ideal time to think through such ideas. You have probably thought through the ethical dimensions of your research all throughout the planning phase, and your approach to the research can often be attributed to ethical issues. This is called action research, and as such, the purpose of the research is to facilitate future positive actions, which is well worth considering in more detail.

Key points in this section:

Thinking through the ethical complexities of research gives us as the researcher time to think about many important aspects of the research process.

Power in the research process

One of the major concerns that a researcher must grapple with is the way that there is a major difference in the balance of power in the research process. Again, this is something that you will have to think through at every stage of your research. The consideration of power relations is very much tied up with the choice of methods, the choice of research question, right through to how you present your research (Karnieli-Miller, Strier and Pessach, 2009). Following is a list of questions that you may find useful to consider in your analysis of power within your research:

What is your research topic?

What is your research question?

What is your research paradigm?

Who are your participants?

How much control do you want participants to have over the research?

To what extent will you interact with participants?

How do you envision presenting the research?

Much early years research seeks to find out about children's experiences that result from our practice. As such, we need to remember that children are used to doing what they are asked to do by adults, and often they accept this readily and actually seek out adults to 'tell them what to do'. This in itself impacts the research design, children do not differentiate between adults as researchers, adults as teachers or practitioners and adults as 'mummies'. This is a point raised by Rogers and Evans (2008) who found that trying to shake off the children's perceived 'adult' role when trying to be a non-participant observer was very difficult. This in itself therefore raises ethical issues not only about the participants' ability to understand and give permission but also ethical issues around how the researcher should act in any given situation. You need to think your responses through in order to make sure that you protect the participants and, as far as possible, don't compromise the integrity of your research. Early years settings are very unpredictable places, and what you are doing through your research design and your ethical considerations is very much trying to anticipate that unpredictability. Trying to be prepared for as many eventualities as you can reasonably think of. You also need to think through how power, the power that you have as an adult or a colleague or even a manager, might impact the integrity of the research and your quest to find the 'truth'.

Following is a table that you might find useful when analysing the use of power in your research.

What is your research topic?	
What is your research question?	
What is your research paradigm?	
Who are your participants?	
How much control do you want participants to have over the research?	
To what extent will you interact with participants?	

Power in research

In order to help researchers consider the ethical implications of their research, there are guidelines available from:

- EECERA – The European Early Childhood Education Research Association
- BERA – The British Educational Research Association
- The British Sociological Association
- The British Psychological Association

For those researching early years practice, then EECERA is probably the most relevant body as they give specific advice on practice with young children.

In the following section, we will consider the guidelines provided by EECERA and try and simplify them and make them more accessible and meaningful to you and your research.

Ethical guidelines

Concerning ethical issues in educational research, there are clear guidelines presented by EECERA (for research specifically focused on early years education and care). At this early point, it would be worth checking with your supervisor to see which guidelines apply. These guidelines are freely available on the Internet and should be consulted throughout the research process. In what follows, we analyse some of the main ethical issues that the guidelines cover. However, the guidelines themselves should be the main point of reference for the consideration of ethical issues throughout your research.

Ethical guidance centres around five main concepts, which remind researchers that they have responsibilities to five different kinds of 'groups' of people within research. The headings are as follows:

- Responsibilities to participants
- Responsibilities to sponsors, clients and stakeholders in research
- Responsibilities to the community of educational researchers
- Responsibilities for publication and dissemination
- Responsibilities for researchers' well-being and development

Responsibilities to participants

This section is probably most familiar to researchers and is therefore the easiest to conceptualise. Broadly speaking, this section can be divided further into concepts, and it is useful to pay close attention to these concepts during the research process.

An ethic of respect for all persons in the research process including ourselves

This section requires researchers to think of participants as multifaceted people with many competing aspects to their identities. An example of this is the recognition of rights and differences due to age, gender, sexuality, ethnicity, class, nationality, cultural identity, partnership status, disability, faith, political belief and so on. As well as the recognition of individual identity traits, researchers should also take account of structural inequalities in the way that different people occupy different spaces in society due to race, gender, disability, sexuality, economic status and so on. The setting of the data gathering should be considered within the context of the overall research.

Research that draws upon social media as a tool to enact the research is becoming more and more popular. However, such research generates many more ethical complexities and these need to be considered. For example, how much can we really tell about participants in online fora (Sugiura, Wiles and Pope 2017) and if the same level of consent obtainable? If as researchers we are given access to data obtained by another organisation, to what extent can we achieve an optimal level of consent? The guidelines also state that researchers must keep up with changes in data use regulations and advice. Researchers should refer to one of the foundational concepts of research ethics. How can the research maximise the benefits and minimise the risk of harm to all involved? Furthermore, it is argued that ethics should be considered at an early stage to think through the possible risks and benefits for all those involved in the research. Any predictable disadvantage of potential harm should be disclosed to participants (or responsible others) at the outset of the research, and steps should be taken to ensure that research does not advantage one group of participants over another.

So, for example, if you are wanting to try out a new pedagogical tool that you think will be advantageous to children, is it ethical to select only a specific group to be part of the research?

The rights of individuals should be viewed alongside any potential social benefits of the research. Researchers need to also account for the complex nature of the lives of those involved in research. For example, researchers need to consider the workload of participants as well as the potentially unforeseen nature of research, which may require renewed consent from participants, gatekeepers, sponsors and so on. When researchers progress towards completing their research, careful thought should be given to the way that participants are informed of the outcomes of the research. This could be particularly important in research that is carried out for the benefit of the participants, such as emancipatory or action research.

Consent and the right to withdraw

In most cases, it is expected that the voluntary informed consent of participants will be gained at the outset of the study and that participants retain the right to withdraw at any point in the research. It should be remembered that within research that fully anonymises participant responses (where the researcher remains unsure as to the identity of the participant), the right to withdraw at any point in the research is not possible. When gaining the consent of participants, everything must be done to ensure that participants understand their involvement in the research, including the possibility of secondary use of research data. The concept of mutual trust (trust between the participant and the researcher) is important here, as well as the integrity of the researcher. The wider setting(s) of the research should be considered, especially when deciding whether a gatekeeper needs to be contacted before directly contacting participants.

This is particularly relevant when online research is concerned. Can participants be contacted directly or is it best to work with gatekeepers such as web hosts or group conveners?

Researchers should be aware of the way that the use of secondary data is often problematic in that the data may have originally been produced with a very different purpose in mind. Does informed consent need to be gained? Is it possible to gain informed consent? Therefore, is the research ethical? Sometimes it is simply impossible to gain consent. However, it is important to document all attempts to gain consent. In the case of group consent, where some members of the group do not consent to the research, practical solutions need to be found, and it should be clearly stated how the research will proceed. For example, in situations where group behaviour is the focus of the research, there may be some individuals who do not consent to involvement in the research. How can these individuals' contributions to the group dynamic be ignored? It should be extended that researchers do not have a singular identity, and thought needs to be given as to the most effective way of conducting research. For example, if a teacher is researching the effectiveness of their teaching, then issues such as power relations, etc., demand careful consideration. When research involves auto/biographical approaches (such as reflections on previous practice), individuals who are not directly involved in the study may still be identifiable, and therefore consent may need to be sought. If the research is carried out by a UK researcher, but the research is generated overseas, the same ethical principles apply, and thorough consideration should be given to how these ethical principles can be applied given the differences in culture. It is almost certain that your guidelines will recognise the United Nations Convention on the Rights of the Child (UNCRC) (1989), and in all cases, researchers will consider the best interests of the child. This is decided by those who have legal responsibility for participants.

Additionally, this is particularly relevant for participants whose age, mental capacity or other vulnerable circumstances mean that others have legal responsibility for their welfare. This often involves gaining consent from parents, guardians and so on. Although opt-in/opt-out procedures for gaining consent are generally acceptable, all local laws concerning opt-in/opt-out research must be adhered to, and researchers are encouraged to be mindful of participants trust in the overall research. For example, an endorsement from a gatekeeper may be considered applicable.

Papatheodorou et al. (2012) suggest that as an early years researcher then ethically although the parents of the child can say that the child can participate, researchers should use every means possible to explain the research so that the child understands and can have a voice and choice in whether or not they agree. They suggest that as a researcher in early years practice, children who are not yet able to read, information should be provided in pictorial format. So you would need to explain your role (if they don't already know), why you are doing research, what you are going to do and what you will do with your learning. Often students explain to children that as well as being with them, they also go to a school to learn and they use pictures of the university to explain where they go, and they show them the classrooms and pictures of them with their fellow students.

Papatheodorou et al. (2012, p. 56), in considering the research method of observation, say you should reassure children of the following:

- If they do not like being observed, they do not need to agree.
- If they have agreed to be observed, you will ask them again every time you do so. This is the process known as receiving the child's assent, rather than the one-off consent that is required from adults.
- You have spoken to their parents and they have agreed to the observation, but explain that the child can still refuse to be observed.
- You will discuss the observations with your teacher/tutor to learn more about children and you may share these observations with them, the child's parents and teachers.
- Photographs will only be taken if the children and their parents agree to this.

Transparency and incentives

Researchers should seek to be open and honest with participants and all stakeholders. It is possible to be granted permission to carry out research on a non-disclosure basis, but this can be particularly tricky. Generally speaking, for research at the undergraduate level, this is discouraged. In cases where research may be sponsored or commissioned, this should be made clear to participants and all stakeholders. Research in which researchers have a conflict of interest, that is where they may stand to gain commercially from the research, is also not appropriate. The use of any incentives to encourage participation should be offered in good sense and should not impinge on the free decision to participate. The use of any incentives should be clearly acknowledged in any reports.

An example of this would be if you were asking co-workers to participate in your research and you brought them a cup of coffee. This would be good sense rather than a major inducement to participate.

Harm

Ethical research seeks to ensure that participation does not result in excessive demands. The notion of not doing any harm has to be factored into any decisions regarding research design and should be monitored throughout the research process. An example of the requirement for thorough consideration of harm is the consideration of the vulnerability of participants. The greater the vulnerability of participants, the greater the responsibility of researchers to ensure that no harm is caused. The issue of time should be thoroughly considered in the design phase of research. This might well render certain research designs unrealistic for undergraduate research; for example, research that involves repeated surveying. The workload that participants must endure should be considered, especially with vulnerable or over-researched participants. Teachers in university cities can often find the constant requests from students overwhelming and, as such, might not be overly enthusiastic. Don't take any rejections personally; just think about how it is from the proposed participants' perspective and try to adapt your methodology and methods if you are finding your proposed participants hard to reach. A conversation with your supervisor would be a good idea.

Privacy and data storage

It is usual practice for the confidentiality and anonymity of participants to be protected during the research process (please see the sample forms later in the chapter). However, it should be remembered that in some cases, participants wish to be identified and researchers should recognise this right. Furthermore, it may be in some contexts and cases impossible to retain anonymity. This is particularly prominent in research conducted within small, close-knit communities.

This can also be an issue when researching well-known institutions and with certain methods, for example, autoethnographic research published under the researchers' name. During the research, any changes to the degree of anonymity that is afforded to participants should be monitored, and the relevant ethics committee may need to be re-consulted. Researchers also need to be aware that the reuse of data may occur even after the initial project is finished. This will also need to be considered and is especially a concern with visual and participatory research. Researchers need to be aware that protecting the privacy of participants must be considered a fluid idea, and researchers must beware that situations might change. For example, some sponsors of research require data to be shared, and researchers may need to consider how they will deal with such requests; this is unlikely to be the case in terms of your research.

Participants' involvement in the project could also be inferred, so researchers may need to consider strategies such as fictionalising data or changing identifying features of participants. The issue of privacy is particularly relevant in research that uses digital contexts. Researchers must ensure that participants' level of understanding of policies, in particular online spaces, is accurate. Researchers should also consider the circumstances in which they would be obligated to report information to the relevant authorities. This is important when considering safe-guarding.

Researchers should always be upfront and honest when informing participants how their data might be used. Judgements also need to be made when visual data or issues such as the recognition of the participant's voice may cause problems regarding anonymity. In addition, legal frameworks regarding data protection must be adhered to. An example of this is the General Data Protection Regulations and your university will more than likely have a Data Protection Officer. You should consult them via your supervisor if in doubt about any aspects of data protection. Researchers must make sure that any data are kept secure.

Things to think about here are:

- the storage of research data,
- use of password protection and data encryption in electronic spaces,
- use of laptops and USB sticks and again password protection,
- moving data (including by email) and the use of third parties in the research. For example, using a transcription service for your interviews.

Disclosure and safeguarding

Before making any judgements concerning the disclosure of participant behaviour to relevant authorities, the confidentiality and anonymity agreements must be considered. There are certain things (such as abuse, proposed acts of terror, etc.) that research shows we are duty-bound to disclose to authorities. Your supervisor should be your first point of contact in situations such as this if you are not researching in your workplace. If you are conducting the research where you work, then you follow the normal procedures for that setting. Participants need to know that confidentiality may be broken if you feel that something that they disclose puts them or others at risk of harm. Wherever you are conducting your research, you need to make sure that you are aware of the organisation's safeguarding policies and procedures and indicate this in your ethics submission, showing that you agree to follow them.

Responsibilities to sponsors, clients and stakeholders in research

Much of this applies to funded research, which is unfortunate for undergraduate dissertations; however, we have had occasions whereby senior management of academy chains has tried to control the research work of their employees to further the work of the organisation and has used the funding of the release time for the student to justify this. However, it should be noted that for funded research, written contracts are the norm and should cover the purpose of the research, the research methods, any conditions of access to your participants, ownership of the data, what researchers want to publish, requirements for reporting and dissemination and any deadlines.

What is perhaps more relevant is the way that the host of the research should be informed of the intentions of the researchers (this would apply to a group of practitioners wishing to conduct research as part of curriculum renewal or development).

Responsibilities to the community of educational researchers

All those who engage in educational research have a responsibility to maintain the integrity and reputation of the discipline by making sure that all research is conducted to the highest standards. It should be noted that critical analysis and constructive criticism are key parts of the enhancement of knowledge; this is different from unfounded criticism or defamatory and unprofessional comments. Another key part of this process is the provision of the contact details of an appropriate person who can be contacted to raise any concerns or formal complaints about the research. Researchers should always endeavour to make their data and methods available for scrutiny, but it is paramount that limitations imposed by confidentiality and anonymity agreements are adhered to. This is particularly important for published research.

Avoiding plagiarism

The guidelines define the act of plagiarism as 'the unattributed use of text and/all data, presented as if they were by the plagiarist' (p. 30). This definition comes from the (2008) committee on publication ethics (Cope) guidelines. Researchers should be aware that issues of plagiarism also apply to the use of digital content.

Researchers have full responsibility for checking the permission rights for the material they reproduce and making sure that it is properly attributed to the source. Remember that if you cite any text word for word, then you must put that text in speech marks and give the author(s), date of publication and page number of the words that have been copied immediately before or after the direct quote. Often, students fall foul of this requirement by omitting the page number when they have used the source material's exact words (rather than a paraphrase, which also needs to be attributed to the source but without the requirement for a page number).

For example.

'Writing offers an exciting opportunity to present findings and interpretations from your observations to other people' (Papatheodoro et al. 2012, p. 150). This is a direct citation as I have used the same words as the original text.

Papatheodoro et al. (2012) say that we should be excited to share our accounts of our observations. This is an indirect citation where I have paraphrased the original text and this does not require a page number as I have interpreted their words.

Responsibilities for publication and dissemination

Much of the guidelines regarding publication and dissemination are largely not applicable to undergraduate dissertations. However, researchers may have a responsibility to make the results of their research public for the benefit of educational institutions and policymakers. In such cases, research should be communicated in a clear and straightforward way. All major contributors to research publications should be acknowledged. Please note that in cases where research is carried out with co-researchers, publication should not be produced without the consent of co-authors; this might occur in a rare circumstance where universities allow joint submissions by candidates. In cases of publication, the forum in which the research is published should be commensurate with the needs and interests of the communities that were involved in the research.

Sometimes your supervisor might wish to work with you on getting your work published. It is worth asking them about possible publication opportunities if you wish to disseminate your work further. Universities often store student projects in their libraries so that the work is available publicly. Many universities have a conference whereby students can choose (or, in some instances, may be required) to share their research.

Responsibilities for researchers' well-being and development

Institutions and sponsoring organisations (such as employers) have a responsibility for safeguarding the physical and psychological well-being of researchers. This may involve an in-depth risk assessment being conducted. For undergraduate dissertation students, it is advised that conversations regarding well-being should be had with your supervisor prior to completing fieldwork.

The carrying out of research can be stressful, and sometimes, despite meticulous planning, unexpected events happen and the project has to be rethought. The students who were completing their projects in 2020 certainly had to navigate a whole raft of new challenges due to the COVID pandemic. Whilst we would hope that you will not encounter such extreme challenges, it is worth remembering that all methodologies can be adapted, and certainly the creativity and thinking outside the box shown by the 2020 students opened new possibilities both in terms of research and general working practices. The advancement of communication and meeting strategies via Teams and Zoom, for instance, created and developed the information and communication skills of the population both nationally and internationally, so maybe we learn new skills from adversity.

This chapter has attempted to simplify the process of gaining ethical approval for your research. It must be said that most ethical procedures simply ensure that you apply common sense throughout your research, and the paper by Banks (2009) highlights how professionals always operate under a code of ethics, the ethics of professional life. You should therefore see the consideration of this as something that should be used to enhance your research rather than something you should fear. If you are at all confused, please consult the relevant guidelines and have a discussion with your supervisor, who will be able to advise you on the right course of action.

References

Banks, S. (2009). From Professional Ethics to Ethics in Professional Life: Implications for Learning, Teaching and Study. *Ethics and Social Welfare*, *3*(1). pp. 55–63.

Committee on Publication Ethics. *Guidelines on Good Publication and the Code of Conduct.* Available from: http://www.publicationethics.org.uk/guidelines.

Convention on the rights of the child. (1989). Treaty No. 27531. *United Nations Treaty Series*, *1577*, pp. 3–178. Available at: https://treaties.un.org/doc/Treaties/1990/09/19900902%2003-14%20AM/Ch_IV_11p.pdf.

Karnieli-Miller, O., Strier, R., & Pessach, L. (2009). Power Relations in Qualitative Research. *Qualitative Health Research*, *19*(2), 279–289.

Papatheodorou, T., Luff, P., & Gill, J. (2012). *Child Observation for Learning and Research.* Routledge.

Rogers, S., & Evans, J. (2008). *Inside Role-Play in Early Childhood Education: Researching Young Children's Perspectives* (3rd ed.). Taylor & Francis Group.

Sugiura, L., Wiles, R., & Pope, C. (2017). Ethical Challenges in Online Research: Public/Private Perceptions. *Research Ethics*, *13*(3–4), 184–199.

Writing the literature review

Kate Firks

What is the overall purpose of the literature review?

A successful literature review demonstrates that you have comprehensive knowledge of a wide, targeted reading base. It allows you to show your very secure understanding of the key scholarly materials, legislation, practitioner-oriented literature and professional reports that are relevant to your chosen topic. This situates your study within past research (O'Leary, 2021) but also builds arguments and critiques methods used in that research (Punch, 2006).

Perhaps unsurprisingly, given the title of this section of the dissertation, the literature forms the basis of the comments that you will make. In-depth critical analysis will be evidenced by well-supported arguments and discussion of pertinent themes (Biggam, 2011) and this will be achieved by synthesising or pulling together numerous well-chosen sources. Rather than aiming to list your opinions and then seek out sources that match them, the review employs literature as the core starting point for the arguments that you want to make. You can certainly express your own thoughts in this part of the dissertation, but its function is primarily to provide the reader with a picture of the existing knowledge of the subject you have chosen and of major questions related to it (Bell, 1999).

First steps

Once students have narrowed the scope of their research and have a working title, they are faced with what may feel like mountains of sources. Having many potential avenues for reading can be very disconcerting, but it is a good sign that shows you are considering your research focus in the widest sense. Starting to write the literature review at this very early stage is a bad idea for this very reason. To begin with, the writing will likely move well away from any intended research focus very swiftly. Secondly, the chapter will probably end up as a 'broad brush' effort, lacking sufficient depth, nuance and criticality and omitting key sources. Finally, if choices about the areas for discussion within the literature review section are not thought through very carefully, the chapter will probably end up disconnected from your research data, making it difficult to make links to the literature base when you are drawing conclusions. For these reasons, preparation and planning for this chapter are key.

Organising your time

Completing the literature review, a significant chapter of the dissertation, involves much sourcing, reading and organising before you get started with any writing. Even after completion, there must be re-drafting and proofreading. The emergence of comprehensive online repositories has meant that a phenomenal amount of material is now immediately accessible at the click of a button. This can feel overwhelming unless you employ strategies with which you can maximise efficiency whilst at the same time demonstrate in-depth engagement with the sources. A tactical, organised and methodical approach must be exercised from the outset.

A little and often approach to the reading (and, later, the writing) is beneficial and more realistic for many people, rather than allocating infrequent whole days or half days. For some people, of course, timeslots will have to be more fixed due to personal commitments. As we will see, effective scaffolding and note-taking really help in this respect, as you can dip in and dip out without spending a long time working out where you were when you last worked on it. It can be very helpful to always keep a notebook or mobile phone voice recording app to hand for the moments when you are doing another activity and suddenly think of something that will work within the dissertation or when you are researching for another assessment and come across a source that links perfectly to your literature review.

Getting going with the reading

Students working on written assignments sometimes report that they dislike spending time on planning of any kind because it feels 'wasted' as it doesn't feel as though it contributes to the essay. Yet not only does it reap considerable benefits in terms of efficiency, but planning your literature review with care before you get going also means you will have the opportunity to talk about the envisaged themes with your supervisor. This is invaluable, as they may offer pertinent suggestions about what should be brought in and what can be left out.

It is therefore sensible, at the earliest stages, to outline the core themes that you think are most relevant. This way, you will be approaching the reading in a targeted and selective manner. Be prepared, however, to add in themes as they appear, as the more you read, the more you will find other relevant issues to consider. This is entirely to be expected, and it shows that you are engaging meaningfully with your reading base.

Locating sources

This may seem obvious, but it is surprising how many students forget that there is much helpful material easily available via their course pages online. One of the first things you should do is re-visit the suggested reading lists and any signposted documents for all relevant modules within your course. This is recommended even if you feel that the chosen area of research for your dissertation is different from anything covered within your programme: it would be a shame to neglect easily accessible information that staff have already signposted for you. In addition, there may be references to theory, practice guidance and underpinning generic policies that will be invaluable in the context of your dissertation. If you have written an essay that touched, however briefly, on aspects of your chosen topic, then also look back closely at the reference lists that you compiled for this, together with any markers' comments about your sources and the ways in which they were employed in your previous work.

Using your initial themes as a guide, make a note of the key words to use within your institution's library catalogue, other databases and search engines. These are not just the words that appear in your dissertation title. If you are looking for a specific theory or pedagogical approach, use the exact wording; otherwise, be prepared to try a wide range of different search terms. For example, if you are exploring issues to do with dyslexia, there will be literature located under terms such as 'special educational needs', 'specific learning difficulties', 'inclusion', 'reading difficulties', 'writing difficulties', etc.

If you have ever used a search engine to find something extremely specific, then you will know that it can take a long time to get what you need – and the most useful weblinks are very rarely the first ones suggested. The same is true when searching for sources for academic work. Students sometimes feel, incorrectly, that because they are having to sift through long lists of suggestions, they must be doing something wrong. Remember that even very experienced researchers will have to spend a great deal of time looking through databases. They will fully expect to have to try a wide number of search terms, adding key words and synonyms. They will allow plenty of time in which to do this, and you will need to factor this in too.

Much time is always needed, but frustrations can be eased by using the numerous system filters in online library databases. If you are unfamiliar with these, have a go at using various filters and check with your institution's library staff if you remain unsure. Sometimes third-year undergraduates feel embarrassed that they do not understand how to effectively use their university library. Now is the time to swallow your pride and seek advice. At a basic level, the filters will allow you to isolate, for example, academic books only, journal articles only, or electronic books only. There will be filters that address the language and date. There will be an option to search for a particular author or title. Your library database may even allow you to look through past students' dissertations; the reference lists in these can be extremely helpful for signposting material as well as for guidance relating to structure and content.

You will have the option to choose the 'full text' of a source in a library database. This is obviously advantageous in that the whole of the material will be made accessible. Attempting to incorporate discussion of a source into a literature review without having viewed it all is not a good idea, as there is a danger that you will understand the material at a superficial level only.

Many students will wish to prioritise materials that address the United Kingdom context or one of the countries within the UK, so filtering findings by geographical location is useful. Bear in mind, however, that there will probably also be relevant sources that relate to theory and research that emanate from other countries. Such overarching international discussions can be invaluable, but there may be texts, or parts of texts, that are too country-specific to be of use, so you will need to use your judgement wisely. As an example, information provided in a piece of German research about strategies to support autistic children may be entirely relevant to an aspect of your dissertation, but some elements, such as specific details of the curriculum and the legislative frameworks for special education, will probably not be (unless you are adopting a comparative approach).

Significant changes can take place in education and early years policy over a few short years. You will want to demonstrate an in-depth understanding of the current practice, so aim to use material that is no older than 7–10 years where you can. Ensure you have accessed the most recent incarnations of legislation and practitioner guidelines. The exceptions to the rule about recent dates are core or seminal theory, which may be considerably dated but has lasted the test of time and is still often cited in new research. Make sure that you date all sources as the time context is important. When writing up, be mindful, too, of chronology – you cannot say that the writer of a source from 2019 'agrees with' the author of a source from 2022!

Research situated in specialties that are considerably different from education (such as business or nursing) or that comes from very context-specific international events (e.g. a conference for Indonesian educators about their approach to their history curriculum) is usually best avoided. Bringing in evidence uncritically does nothing to demonstrate that you have worked to ensure your literature base is relevant – and can, frankly, make the marker feel that the student has used the first thing that came to hand in order to quickly 'backfill' a point they are making. You will want to show the marker that you have paid great attention to the scope and quality of the sources that you have chosen to include. This is very important.

Types of sources

References to literature act to show you understand your topic in depth, provide justification for your arguments, allow you to compare and contrast current research, and help you to express ideas in a suitably formal way. Different institutions, different degree courses and different supervisors will all have differing approaches to what constitutes an 'acceptable source', so, first, make sure you are very clear about the requirements and outline with your supervisor what types of material you should and should not use. *If in any doubt, always check with them.*

Despite these differences, all literature reviews will, in the main, be comprised of three types of text. You are likely to have had plenty of experience with each of these over the course of your degree. They will comprise *primary source material*, like most journal articles (where the people who did the research/developed the theory are writing about it) and *secondary source material* (where the writer is reporting what others have done/said).

1. **Books** form the bedrock of much scholarly (or 'academic') work and will be vital in the literature review. These will usually have been published by university presses, professional bodies and commercial publishing houses. Unlike journal articles, which mainly detail individual pieces of research and usually focus narrowly, books are usually broader in scope. They are vital for key theories and wider arguments. Academic books will also contain a list of references, or a bibliography, and these can be used to signpost you to further useful texts. Increasingly, books are available as electronic books via online library databases, thus reducing the requirement to take out physical copies. There are also extremely useful search options within the format that help when it comes to finding key words and key chapters. That said, there are many good reasons to visit your library in person: scanning the relevant sections of paper copies is quick, a look around nearby shelves may reveal much interesting material that you would otherwise have neglected and there may be options to obtain texts via an inter-library loan.

    Academic textbooks are often not read in their entirety or chronologically, as the index will indicate the relevance of the content to your study. Textbooks are written in formal language, contain technical terms, are often lengthy, can be intimidating in their depth and tone, and rarely lend themselves to light bedtime reading. Being able to use them efficiently is vital; it may be that just one section, sentence or statistic is applicable to the topic of study. So, access the outline of the text online or in the blurb, and then use the Contents and Index pages to ascertain whether the text will be useful for your purpose.

    Be very wary of accessing a source that is only a small part of a book chapter (an example is the kind of very brief extract found on a bookseller's commercial website). There is a danger here that you will miss a key contextual element or other significant detail.

2. **Journal articles** are aplenty online, and the advent of open access repositories has widened the scope further. Many journals do still require a subscription, but your university library will pay for many of these, which is why your institution's library catalogue should always be your first port of call. Some of the journal articles will be available in their entirety, and this is always preferable. Other articles will be hidden behind paywalls elsewhere. It is worth checking to see if you can use your institution's access to get to them, so try

other databases, for example the ERIC research database and the EBSCOhost Research Platform. Research Gate is often a good platform to consult if you know that a particular author has a body of work that relates to your study. On Research Gate, the author will often make their work available free of charge.

There is much literature available on the wider internet, but some students avoid their library's database altogether, which is counter-intuitive, given that their lecturers will have had considerable input into the books and journals held there. There should be no need at all to pay for articles, and your dissertation supervisor is not going to expect you to undertake a huge search for a single minor text. Overall, your review will end up containing a wealth of material, so one obscure article is very likely to make little difference. If you feel that a paper that is not currently available to you is essential to furthering your study, then most institutions offer a set number of free interlibrary loans, whereby they source the paper for you from another academic library. Avoid using abstruse sources as a way of trying to impress your marker; they will want to see that you have read relevant and current discourse and debate – the 'core body' of the literature – rather than peculiar, peripheral material. You will not be reinventing the wheel in your dissertation and many experienced academics will have explored similar themes to you (Walliman, 2013).

Increasingly, paywalls are being removed and open-access academic research is available. This means that the material has been freely shared online, removing the need for an individual or organisation to pay to view it. Google Scholar is freely available to all and has a variety of options when it comes to searching. Even if the original source is not needed for your purpose, it may be that its list contains links to a source that could be, so checking others' reference lists is eminently sensible.

3. **Other sources**

'Grey literature' is that which has not been published by commercial publishers in books or journals. Broadly speaking, this includes information such as conference proceedings, committee reports: government reports (e.g. those published by the Department for Education); policy documents and statistics; doctoral (PhD) theses: practice guidelines; practitioner-oriented literature; academics' blogs; reports from non-governmental organisations; reports from professional bodies; and research groups and preprints (journal articles that are yet to be peer-reviewed or published). Grey literature is often very current and can be particularly useful when it comes to policies and statistics. It also allows a wider range of voices to be heard, as not everyone who has something useful to say publishes with commercial publishers. It is vital to bear in mind that much grey literature has not been peer-reviewed, so you will need to use your judgement when bringing in into your writing.

For some other online grey literature related to education topics, you could try OpenDOAR (open access repositories), BASE – Bielefeld Academic Search

Engine (much open access material), OpenGrey (grey literature in Europe) and WorldCat (a collection of library catalogues).

If you are arguing the social and/or scientific significance of a point that you are making, you may wish to incorporate material that sits outside of research. Statistics, debates and controversies can appear in **popular media coverage** (O'Leary, 2021). As a rule of thumb, if the reports on news websites, education websites such as the Times Educational Supplement or within social media posts mention research, you are expected to find the original research rather than use the website as your reference. However, if you wish to explore how the media are covering an issue, or want to show public opinion and current disputes, referencing popular media can enhance arguments.

Additional notes on quality

Peer-reviewed journal articles have gone through a process of evaluation whereby journal editors and other experts have read and critically assessed the quality of the research and the article itself. They have determined that the data presented is **reliable** (i.e., with measurements that are consistent) and **valid** (the research measures what it claims to). If you are using a database to find articles, you can limit the search to peer-reviewed sources. Some sections within scholarly journals, such as letters to the editor and book reviews, will not have been peer-reviewed. All peer-reviewed articles are classified as scholarly, but it is worth noting that not all scholarly sources (e.g., reports from government departments) will have been peer-reviewed. Consider, too, the **credibility** of your chosen text. Is the article from a reputable academic journal? Is it recent? Are the methods used logical? Are the conclusions accurate? Are arguments made appropriate? *Always check with your supervisor if you are unsure whether you should be using a source.*

A discussion of theoretical perspectives will need to be present and *must* be based on the examination of books and journal articles and not on media reports or other non-peer-reviewed sources. Ideally, the discussion of theory should come from the incorporation of work by the original theorist and the evaluation of their ideas by other academic authors. In a similar vein, most early years-focused dissertations will include discussion of government legislation and guidance, for example, the SEND Code of Practice 0–25 Years (Department for Education & Department of Health, 2015), Ofsted Research Reviews and the Teachers' Standards (Department of Education, 2011). Read any brief summaries to assist with your understanding, but for the literature review, you will be expected to have engaged with the original source.

In a similar way, aim to avoid secondary references (where you use a source that is cited in someone else's book or journal article). Incorporating material second-hand appears to the marker as though you have not bothered to find and read the primary source. It also prevents you from showing that you have fully understood the text, reducing the impact of the arguments made, and can even act as a flag for possible plagiarism. Of course, sometimes an original text is no longer in print, but secondary referencing is not good academic practice and it is imperative to show you have engaged with the authors' original ideas.

'Remember that there is a lot of rubbish on the internet' (Davies & Hughes, 2014 p.39). Never has a truer word been spoken! You must prioritise the very best sources and arguments are weakened by a lack of care and discrimination with source material.

Managing the material

It is inadvisable to routinely print off whole journal articles or book chapters. You will be accessing such an extensive number of texts and the likelihood is that you will end up with pages upon pages to file and then will be forced to sift through it all for a single statistic or quote. Printing is also time-consuming and expensive, and is not good from an environmental perspective. If something appears particularly attractive because it contains a wealth of information and signposts to texts (for example, an article that is itself a comprehensive literature review of your chosen subject area), then it can of course be printed off if needed, but aim not to habitually default to paper versions. If you like using paper copies because you are keen on highlighting, this can just as easily be done on PDFs and other file types and has the advantage of being readily available in multiple locations if stored on a cloud-based filing system.

Do not be intimidated by your source. It is common for research articles to contain a multitude of technical terms and a considerable amount of complex data. The chances are that these elements are not the parts of the source that are most useful for you. The literature review is about an overview of your topic as opposed to an analysis of the minutiae of an individual piece of research.

You will need to become efficient at getting through copious quantities of literature speedily to ascertain their worth to your topic. This can be made easier by skimming and scanning.

- *Skimming* is about reading selectively rather than ploughing through the entirety of a source. The publication date, introduction, any summaries, the first and last sentences in paragraphs, anything in bold type, headings, charts of graphs, etc. will offer vital elements. You may want to cover the finer points at a later stage, but when sourcing texts, you need to be able to decide on relevance quickly. You will still need to concentrate on what you are doing, as skimming is reading actively; a lack of attention will lead to missing key elements or to misinterpretation.

- *Scanning* is different in that instead of obtaining a good overview, you are looking for specific pieces of information. We tend to do this often as part of our daily lives, for example, when we look at a bus timetable or through a magazine or website to find something specific. When scanning, the aim is to see if certain words are present. As an example, you might want to find a particular piece of legislation, such as the Children and Families Act 2014, or the name of a particular theorist. If you are viewing a document online, you may be able to use a document search facility to locate key words quickly.

Recording what you have read

It is imperative to keep a record of your reading as you go and to systematically log it (O'Leary, 2021). It is hugely frustrating and time-consuming to realise that you have a very useful quote but have absolutely no idea where it came from. Keep a copy of your institution's referencing guidance close to hand; it can be helpful to have some examples of how to reference the texts you will repeatedly use (such as books, journal articles and legislation) and to pin this up near your computer screen. Time spent doing this at the note-taking stage will reap considerable rewards at the write-up stage. Seek advice from your supervisor if you have checked all guidance but are still unsure about how to reference a source accurately. This is especially important if you are bringing in types of material, for example, conference proceedings, that you have not needed to reference before.

Reading needs to be recorded carefully. Some students like to fill in summary charts onscreen using a copy-and-paste technique. Others prefer to use 'old-fashioned' index cards. The latter remain useful, as they are portable, can easily be added to, and do not require access to a computer. You can, of course, summarise the contents of individual sources using one card/Word document per text, but this can easily lead to an intimidating heap of disjointed material. One solution is to then take these and sort them into themes, complete with counter-arguments. Another possibility is to arrange index cards/Word documents by themes and counter-arguments from the outset; this focus on embedding literature within identified topics from the beginning can help to prevent unstructured and unfocused paragraphs. An example of a summary document organised thematically can be found in Appendix I.

Booth et al. (2016) make the useful point that distinguishing between *what you have quoted exactly*, *what you have paraphrased* and *your own thoughts* by writing/typing in three different colours will help immensely when you come to synthesising your reading. Embedding clarity in this way will, ultimately, save time and – vitally – will reduce the chance of inadvertent plagiarism.

Getting going with the writing

Once you have read widely and made records of this, it can be tempting to want to get going with the writing element 'properly' with only the roughest of outlines. However, doing so is akin to getting dressed to go on a country walk with no idea of where you are going to go and the route that you will take when you get there! An effective note-taking system for the reading and a firm scaffold for the writing that follows pay dividends in terms of time and reduced stress. Students thankfully no longer must handwrite their work or use typewriters, so the need for working chronologically is much lessened. Ideas for how to go about the overall structure of the literature review are discussed in more detail later in this section.

You will certainly need to render the flow of the chapter logical, but that does not mean that you must write sections in the order that they will appear in the final write-up. Having a secure scaffold in place means that you are later free to write in 'chunks' and can easily manipulate the overall order of the material once individual sections are completed.

Structuring the chapter

In terms of length, the literature review will take up a substantial number of words within the dissertation. Exactly how many will depend upon the guidance that you have been given. Within the chapter will be headings and sub-headings (check if you are allowed to use the latter) that will break the considerable material down into identified themes. Your work may lend itself to a *chronological* structure (for example, if you are looking at the history of a play approach) but it will more likely be *thematic*. Common mistakes are to leap into discussion of the literature without situating it in any kind of context/argument and to create a chapter without paying attention to the overall order of material. Barrow and Westrup (2019, p. 65) call this "a 'shopping list approach'". Having similar, or usefully contrasting, points in entirely different sections also dilutes opportunities to show critical engagement.

Your supervisor will give advice regarding the shape of the chapter, but in general, it will consist of the following:

- An **introduction** that links to the objectives of the research, outlining what you are going to examine and why. You may wish to discuss the kinds of literature that you have chosen to analyse and what you have chosen to leave out.

- **Sections** (with headings and possibly sub-headings) that discuss the literature in defined and relevant themes, showing the relationship between your topic and the literature base. These middle sections form the main body of the chapter and will likely comprise around 80% of the words within it. It can be very helpful to use the first sections to address the wider elements and then move into very focused discussions. As an example, you might discuss how education for early years is organised, then discuss issues related to support for pupils with SEND and then address problems related to effective support for young children with speech, language and communication issues. Each section will comprise several paragraphs and there should be a logical flow from one section to the next so that interrelated connections are made clear for the reader. The wording of any headings can, of course, be changed later, and it may be that you decide to delete some of them completely at the end of the day.

Make sure that at various points you link back to elements of the original research question. If what you are writing has nothing to do with it, you have gone offtrack.

- A **conclusion** that summarises the main findings, responding to the original research aims and appraises the literature on your topic in a general way. You may also wish to mention any areas that you consider under-researched. It is common for students to get carried away and fail to finish the chapter effectively, leaving it 'hanging in the air' and the reader confused as to its function within the wider writing.

- A brief **signpost** to the next chapter (which is the Methodology).

O'Leary (2021) provides a helpful summary of the distinctive styles of writing that you will engage with in the literature review chapter:

- ***Descriptive*** (facts/information)
- ***Analytical*** (organising into logical groupings and comparing/contrasting)
- ***Critical*** (assessing work and ascribing value to show you are engaging with the literature)
- ***Persuasive*** (making informed arguments and showing the significance of your chosen research)

Description versus critical evaluation

Many students will be familiar with assignment feedback that suggests that they work to improve their criticality. In academic writing, being critical is not 'being negative'. *Critical engagement* is about comparing and contrasting a range of perspectives, integrating your quotations and paraphrased information carefully, rather than wasting valuable words describing at copious length what one theorist says or detailing elements of a piece of research that are irrelevant to your overarching points. Neither is it about merely summarising the literature; it should instead situate it within clearly defined arguments.

Resist the urge to begin the first sentence of every paragraph with a reference to literature; it is much better to either make a statement about the topic to signpost the reader or integrate the source within a sentence that clarifies the overarching theme (for example, 'Recent research (Brown, 2022) has contradicted this assertion'). Jesson et al. (2011) suggest that students check the words at the beginning of each paragraph to make sure that they do not begin with the author's name and to ensure that the writing is not merely a series of descriptions of sources presented one after the other. The sequential use of one source in one paragraph is a common fault and does not indicate your understanding to the reader.

There will be times in the writing where you describe key facts and information – no literature review can be without description. But this chapter should explore the common and opposing issues across a range of sources, rather than one source at a time (Barrow and Westrup, 2019). Every citation should have a purpose that is clear to the reader – if a direct quotation or paraphrase is inserted without attention to this the marker will, rightly, think 'So what?'

As part of this critical approach, there will be times when you can also bring in your own view about what you have read, that is, you will *critique your source*. There may be a problem with it that you feel is worth mentioning, e.g. a piece of research might have excluded the views of a key group of people or it may have been undertaken before a new set of practitioner guidelines was published. The literature review may well identify 'gaps' in the research that your dissertation project intends to fill; it may highlight interesting controversies and can also justify your methodological approach, so it can be helpful to highlight any limitations of previous studies (O'Leary, 2021). That said, there is certainly no need to critique the value of every text you use: not only will this reduce the focus on your core arguments and be extremely dull to read, but as an undergraduate researcher, it inevitably comes across as impertinent to repeatedly pass judgement regarding the quality and rigour of the peer-reviewed work of seasoned scholars.

Most of the reading will be synthesised via **paraphrasing**. Keep **direct quotes** (where you have used the exact words within a source) to a minimum and *always* situate them in a context by making clear their relevance. Remember that quotations copied out word-for-word do not show a) that you understand what you have written and b) can *apply* it to a stated argument. They should be used when the author's original words are so pertinent that just paraphrasing will not do. Peppering your writing relentlessly with the words of others, either via direct quotes or paraphrasing, also causes you to lose ownership of your work (as too much has not come from you) and leads to a bitty, 'staccato' effect, whereby the flow of the writing is constantly interrupted by citations.

In addition, multiple in-text references to the same piece of literature within a paragraph can be annoying and are not entirely necessary. If the source is cited and the very next sentence makes it abundantly clear that you are talking about that source (e.g. 'This research concluded that...'), then you do not need to reference it again. If there are to be several more sentences about this source, then ensure another reference is added at the end. When you proofread, if there is any point where you think the reader might be unclear as to which source you mean, add in a reference.

Each paragraph should make a point that is supported by the literature (O'Leary, 2021). If you wish to make the argument that X is the case, then once you have asserted this, you must bring in evidence that academic research and theory support your assertion that X is the case. You might then bring a source that disagrees that X is the case and instead posits that Y is the case. If more than one source makes the same point, this adds weight; bringing in multiple in-text references by different authors will emphasise this. To help develop an analytical approach, you can therefore group sources together to show similarities or put them together to emphasise their differences. Either way, you are using the literature to develop a persuasive argument a) that the reader can follow easily and b) that shows the relevance of your own research.

Jesson et al. (2011) provide a useful list of synonyms that can be used when writing about a text. These show alternative ways of saying similar things and can help avoid repetition:

Account for	Clarify	Describe	Empathy	Investigate	Recognise
Analyse	Compare	Determine	Expand	Judge	Reflect
Argues	Contrast	Discuss	Explain	Justify	Refer to
Assess	Criticise	Distinguish	Exhibit	Narrate	Relate to
Assert	Debate	Differentiate	Identify	Outline	Report
Assume	Defend	Evaluate	Illustrate	Persuade	Review
Claim	Define	Emphasise	Imply	Propose	Suggest
	Demonstrate	Examine	Indicate	Question	Summarise

Academic tone

A literature review requires the same formal style as any other piece of academic writing. Therefore, contractions or colloquialisms should be avoided, and language should be streamlined and precise. Use words that you understand and avoid trying to impress with florid and complex phrasing, as this can get in the way of what you are trying to get across. Steer clear of hyperbole (exaggerating for emphasis, e.g., 'This is a fantastic method for...') and of generalisation (e.g. 'autistic children dislike change').

Also avoid complex/unnecessary shifts in verb tense within a paragraph or adjacent paragraphs. It is likely that you will generally use the present perfect tense (e.g., 'Scientists *posed*') or the present perfect (e.g. 'Researchers *have reported*') or the past tense ('The team *reported*'). If the point you are making is applicable to the present, you can use the present tense as well (e.g. 'The researchers concluded that *this is* not an effective method of support'. The present or future tense is needed where you are signposting the reader to what you intend to do in the writing (e.g., 'The following section *develops* this theme' or 'The next section *will develop* this theme').

In most dissertations, there will be an expectation that the first-person perspective, which primarily uses pronouns such as I and me, and the second-person perspective, which employs pronouns such as you and yours, are avoided. Instead, third-person pronouns (*he, she, it, they, him, her, them, his, her, hers, its, their, and theirs*) need to be used. Common indefinite third-person nouns you will use include *the writer, the reader, individuals, students, people, a person, researchers, scientists, writers* and *experts*.

There are several particularly useful academic phrasebanks available online and possibly also from your institution that will help you with various aspects of phraseology encountered in the writing. These are generally very neutral in nature, and therefore, it does not constitute plagiarism to use or adapt them. A well-known and comprehensive example is that produced by Manchester University at *phrasebank.manchester.ac.uk*.

Plagiarism and academic malpractice

Plagiarism can be an intentional act but may happen completely by accident; either way, it is to be avoided at all costs and can have extremely grave consequences. Your institution will have guidance about plagiarism and they may also employ software such as TurnItIn that checks work for signs of it. Most students are aware that failing to reference a quote is plagiarism. But what may constitute plagiarism is more than just this. A common mistake is to think that putting things into your own words (paraphrasing) means that you can get away without providing a reference to the original. This is presenting another's views as your own – i.e., plagiarism. Another mistake is not paraphrasing enough, i.e., choosing words that are too close to the original. The main ideas must be accurate, but the wording needs to be your own.

A less common, but equally serious, problem is to misrepresent what a source is saying. Here, rather than claiming someone else's work as their own, the result is a falsification of the original in terms of data or author intention. Not only does this show that a student has not read and/or understood what they have referenced, it also has the potential to damage others' reputations and is very definitely classed as academic malpractice. Always show that you have grasped what the source means – apply your knowledge – and seek clarification from your supervisor or locate a different text if you feel you are not able to accurately represent the author's original intentions.

Overcoming writer's block

Many students find that sitting down to a blank screen to write the first few words is intimidating and even stressful. It is natural to feel this way, and even seasoned writers experience the same feelings. The act of writing the very first few sentences can feel as though it highlights the immensity of the task ahead. This is all perhaps more likely with a dissertation, given its length when compared with other assignments students undertake and its traditional importance as a big piece of work at the end of your degree. Writer's block, procrastination and/or anxiety about writing are particular problems with the literature review section, given its significance as the first long chapter and the degree to which synthesis of numerous complex sources is required.

The best way to manage this is to not make a big deal about it! You are not chiselling your words in stone and will inevitably change or remove parts considerably later, so there is no point in wasting energy avoiding making a start. If you have allowed sufficient time to read, to think, to plan, to write (and proofread) and to reference accurately, the act of crafting the chapter will hopefully not be too onerous, and you will still have plenty of time left to make any changes.

To maintain flow and momentum, resist the urge to heavily edit as you go. Anxiety about writing accuracy can be a particular problem for students with dyslexia, who may also have already spent a long time reading a source and composing their work. Repeatedly re-reading the same section of your writing or worrying about individual words or phrases wastes time, causes stress and affects confidence. It is much easier to keep going and edit later. That said, keep an eye on the word count – it is a poor idea to write thousands of extra words and then have to take them all out again! The caveat to the point about not editing as you go is the reference. This is the one part of the writing that is well worth getting accurate as you proceed, both in the text itself and in the final reference list.

If you feel that you are struggling to use your time wisely or are encountering considerable stress when attempting to write, then you must contact your supervisor.

Saving work

It is obvious, but always save work done on a computer very regularly. Saving in the Cloud not only allows you to auto-save your dissertation draft, it also means that you are free to work on it using different computers. Crucially, if your computer's hard drive fails, your machine is stolen or you misplace your memory stick, your work will still be available, preventing much heartache. Whether you use Cloud storage or not, get into the habit of saving your files often, maybe even emailing them to yourself, and when renaming a file, make sure you do so in a way that ensures that you are always working on the latest draft. The last thing you want to do after working so hard on this challenging chapter is waste time editing an outdated incarnation!

Whilst it seems like an onerous task, getting the literature review right sets you up to successfully complete your whole project.

References

Barrow, C., & Westrup, R. (2019). *Writing Skills for Education Students* (3rd ed.). Red Globe Press.

Bell, J. (1999). *Doing Your Research Project: A Guide for First-Time Researchers in Education and Social Science* (3rd ed.). Open University Press.

Biggam, J. (2011). *Succeeding with Your Master's Dissertation: A Step-by-Step Handbook* (2nd ed.). Open University Press.

Booth, W., Colomb, G. G., Williams, J. M., Bizup, J., & Fitzgerald, W. T.. (2016). *The Craft of Research* (4th ed.). University of Chicago Press.

Davies, M., & Hughes, N.. (2014). *Doing a Successful Research Project Using Qualitative or Quantitative Methods* (2nd ed.). Palgrave Macmillan

Department for Education & Department of Health. (2015). *Special educational needs and disability code of practice: 0 to 25 years*. Available at: https://www.gov.uk/government/publications/send-code-of-practice-0-to-25 (Accessed: 09 May 2023).

Department for Education. (2011). *Teachers' Standards*. Available at: https://www.gov.uk/government/publications/teachers-standards (Accessed: 09 May 2023).

Jesson, J. K., Matheson, L., & Lacey, F. M. (2011). *Doing Your Literature Review: Traditional and Systematic Techniques* (3rd ed.). SAGE.

O'Leary, Z. (2021). *The Essential Guide to Doing Your Research Project* (3rd ed.). SAGE.

Punch, K. F. (2006). *Developing Effective Research Proposals* (3rd ed.). SAGE.

Walliman, N. (2013). *Your Undergraduate Dissertation: The Essential Guide for Success* (2nd ed.). SAGE.

Appendix I

Reading summary chart – thematic

Theme (Core ideas found across a range of different sources)	Source 1 (State what the text says about the theme. Look for similar views and contrasting opinions. Add in the full reference).	Source 2	Source 3	Source 4	Key theory?	Issues? Any gaps that need further investigation?

Data collection
Jan Gourd

Introduction

This chapter will look at data collection, the chapter on methodology and methods should have helped you prepare your project and this chapter assumes that you are ready to go after having agreed on your plan with your supervisor. The chapter revisits and extends some of the information in previous chapters, the idea being that you read this as an aide memoire and extension of existing preparation. If you find some of the information repetitive, that is intentional, as it might have been some time since you chose your methods. The purpose of this chapter is to consolidate your thinking and help you through the data collection phase.

Ready to go

Data collection is often the most enjoyable part of the project in that you are involved in an organic situation whereby new perspectives on your area of interest are evolving in front of you. Researchers should approach data collection with sensitivity, openness and flexibility. They should try to collect high-quality data that provides new insights into their research question. The data collection stage is the most crucial stage of the research project.

Data collection can also be frustrating; for example, you have everything planned and what to get on with it, but then you must wait for responses from gatekeepers and other permissions to be gained. You must not commence data collection until you have ethical approval from your university and permissions from the proposed participants and their setting if the research is to be located there.

In many early years research contexts, the student must apply for permission to carry out the research in a specific setting or with a specific group of people. For example, if you want to study and observe how children relate to specific activities, then you will need a series of permissions: permission from the manager of the setting (the gatekeeper), permission from the parents of the children to be observed, permission from any practitioners involved and permission from the children themselves.

Please look at the ethics chapter for more specific detail here. You must also outline how participants can change their mind about being a part of your research and withdraw their data from the study. You can set a date by which time this must be done as you cannot hold on to data analysis forever, and to proceed with the data analysis and then have a request for a specific data set to be extracted are going to take a significant amount of your time in reworking that section of your study.

You have to accept that all this permission gathering does take time and can be frustrating for you, but the procedures are in place to protect you and ultimately to minimise the withdrawal rate of participants. Hamilton and Corbett-Whittier (2012) have a useful section on this, whereby they also remind us that anyone engaging in research with children will need to be cleared by the relevant Criminal Records Board. In the United Kingdom, this is known as a CRB check, and if you are already working in the setting that you are researching in, then you should already have this in place. If the setting does not employ you and you intend to be in the presence of children, then you need to find out from the gatekeeper what they require from you in this regard.

Once you have all the relevant permissions, then you must organise the dates and times for the research to take place. Again, this takes a lot of planning. Sometimes when we are trying to communicate with an organisation, waiting for replies can be frustrating, especially when you are on a time-limited journey; however, researchers must remember that gatekeepers and participants are gifting us their time and so we need to be very grateful and diplomatic in all our communications, no matter how frustrating the situation is for us. Having said that, if you are not getting the answers you need and time is dragging on, you do need to think about either approaching another organisation or setting or modifying the research in some way. Make sure that you share what is happening or not happening with your supervisor, as they can advise you on what to do. Often, students carry on hoping that permissions will be achieved for way too long and then end up compromising their ability to complete the project well. You need to have a final date to achieve access and have a plan B should that not happen. Again, if you need to abstract yourself from a specific setting, you need to manage this professionally and respectfully; again, your supervisor will advise you.

Hopefully everything goes well, and you are ready to proceed with the data collection phase.

Once you are ready to begin, then you need to think about how you are going to handle the data that you collect. We will look at some popular methods of data collection below and think about the preparation needed before the event. These methods might be used in isolation or in combination with other methods to help you answer your research question. Planning within research is everything, and the better prepared you are, then the more useful the data you collect will be to you in your pursuit of new knowledge.

We will now revisit three data collection methods that are widely used by students and consider specifically how the data will be collected in an organised manner.

Observation

This is part of most early years' practitioners' everyday lives. However, in a research context, you need to decide on whether you will be a participant in the scenario to be observed or a non-participant. If you are observing at the place where you work, then hoping to be a non-participant can raise some challenges, as young children are likely to not understand that you are not interacting with them. You also need to decide on how you will collect the data, will you have an observation schedule, or will you provide a narrative account of what you are observing? Are you hoping to capture dialogue or just physical behaviours? Oates and Hey (2014) provide some sound advice on observations and suggest that observations of children can provide very valuable information for evaluating and reflecting on practice. They take care to emphasise the ethical issues around this technique and suggest that the observations should be carefully planned and 'capture as much detail as possible and be factual and accurate' (Oates and Hey 2014, p. 47). If you have chosen observation as a tool, then you will be operating within a constructivist position, and as such, you need to recognise that your assumptions that you bring to the observation will be reflected in your data. It is fine to have assumptions as long as we acknowledge them. Papatheodorou et al. (2011) give extensive advice on all areas of observation in settings. They give advice on:

- Methods of observation – advice on using checklists, time sampling, target child, sociograms, tracking maps, event sampling and narrative observation.

- The planning of observations.

- An explanation of the ethical considerations.

If you are planning on using observation, then this is a comprehensive text, and you will save a lot of time by following the advice as well as gaining some very pertinent citable material for your methodology.

Ingram and Elliott (2020) concentrate on giving advice for collecting data from observation that hopes to capture the dialogue as well as any action. In their chapter on data collection, they discuss audibility in classrooms and shared spaces and suggest that if the dialogue is the most important data, then the naturalness of the everyday place might need to be compromised and a quieter space found to complete the research. These are some of the decisions that have to be made at the planning stage to ensure the best possible conditions for capturing the data. Each decision would involve compromise, as you would probably want to observe children or practitioners in their 'normal/natural' environment but if you are trying to record word for word all the interactions of a specific group, then this might be difficult in the general hubbub of the day-to-day work of the classroom/space. Either choice will be a compromise, and you need to show that you are aware of the implications of your choices when you write up your methodology. So, in one scenario, you risk creating a 'special' event out of the normal parameters of the experience, and in the other, you risk missing key dialogue due to background noise. Of course, ideally every participant would have a microphone and every word would be captured in the natural setting, but that scenario is unlikely in most student research, and even when the technology seems to support the research, there can still be unforeseen circumstances. I remember a colleague explaining her research on children's play and how the target children were equipped with Gopro cameras to wear to record both their actions and dialogue; however, the unforeseen was the speed at which the children moved and hence the blurred images that were achieved.

An interesting discussion of the methodological decisions that we as researchers make when working with young children is discussed in chapter 3 of Rogers and Evans (2008). *Inside role-play in early childhood education: Researching young children's perspectives.* Whilst this book discussed a multi-modal methodology, one of the methods used is observation. The authors take the readers through their decision-making process and reflect on their choices. They also explore the difficulties of the children's perceptions and the roles they assigned to the researchers who sought to be as non-participating as possible in the research setting.

Once you are ready and clear about the purposes of using observation as a tool, then you need to decide on how you will anonymise any notes that you keep so that should you lose them, the participants are not identifiable.

So, if you are planning to use the method of observation as a research tool, use the following checklist to help plan your data collection.

- Have I got a clear purpose for the observation, have I isolated the variables that I want to observe?
- Have I decided on where and when the observation will take place?
- Have I arranged enough time to complete the observation?
- Have I got all the relevant permissions in writing/email?
- Am I clear about how I will complete the observation with due regard to ethical guidelines?
- Am I clear on the observation protocol that may already exist in the setting? Is what I intend to do consistent with this?
- Am I clear about the coding (maybe pseudonyms) I will use to anonymise data collected?
- Do I have a clear idea of how I am going to collect the data, e.g., do I have a schedule? Are there specific time samples that I will use, e.g., record what participant A is doing every five minutes or am I looking holistically at everything that happens?
- Am I clear about how I am going to record the data?

If photographs are involved, do I have and am I clear that all the relevant permissions have been gained?

Data storage

You need to collect and organise the data gathered carefully being mindful of any anonymity you may have promised and keeping the data safe and secure. Hamilton and Corbett-Whittier (2012) have a useful chapter on this, which emphasises the use of digital recording equipment as part of observation and the ethical issues associated with the managing, storing and eventual disposal of the data. Their advice is specific to case study methodology, but the general principles can be applied across most scenarios. They note that careful organisation of data is necessary to ensure the coherence of the analysis. In the case of a sequence of observations, for example, you will probably want to store these chronologically to see the development over time of a specific variable that you are seeking to observe. For instance, if you are looking at the social interactions of a specific target child, over the course of three weeks, it is obvious that you need to date and time stamp these observations, but these are often the small details that are overlooked, and students often compromise their research by not rigorously organising the data they have collected. What seems obvious gets overlooked in the chaos of the moment, particularly if the student researcher also works in the setting being researched and their 'day job' switches to be their focus shortly after they have been completed a session of data collection. Be aware of this and have some means of immediately storing the data logically; for example, if your observations have been narrative and handwritten, then immediately insert them into a dated cardboard file. This level of organisation will save you time and provide for more robust analysis that will ultimately lead to a better grade. It isn't just what you write and hand in that contributes to the grade; your organisation of data collection will be evident through your methodology and data analysis sections and will therefore contribute to your overall grade.

Interviews

As with all forms of data collection, interviews take planning. Interviews can be time-consuming, but they also have the potential to produce very rich data. The considerations are many and include the time of the interview. If your interviews are with practitioners, think about when and where they are to take place. You need to always remember that your participants are doing you a favour. They are giving some of their time to you, so you need to be flexible in meeting their needs; for example, the 15 minutes just after the children have left might not be the best time. You need to think about when your participants will be able to spare the time to talk with you as unburdened as possible from their ordinary work time (unless, of course, you are seeking to research practitioner wellbeing or responses to critical incidents, in which case, authentic 'in the moment' responses might suit your research aims). It is also worth considering the location for the interview; considerations could be the potential interruptions if held within the place of work or the inconvenience of travelling somewhere else. If the chosen location is a public place, then what about background noise. Often, students invite their colleague research participants to come to their place of study to be interviewed, therefore distancing themselves and the participant from the naturalised environment. There are obviously implications either way, but colleagues often like to see 'where you disappear to on Fridays' and the change of venue gives a sense of your different role as researcher in this moment. A change of venue can be helpful in defining the conversation as research rather than reflection, and whether that matters or not will depend upon your research question. If you do decide to move out of the participants setting, make sure that you have secured a space and have given the participants sufficient details, for example, over parking, finding the room, etc., and sufficient time to get there. Again, planning is key, and the more detailed the plan, the better the outcome should be in terms of successfully completing your project or dissertation.

Hamilton and Corbett-Whittier (2012) provide a useful guide to planning interviews and they suggest that you pilot your interviews before committing to collecting data. They stress that piloting an interview will help to highlight any ambiguity there is within the proposed questions so that this can be addressed prior to conducting the interview with the research participants. They also alert us to the fact that some communication is non-verbal and ask us to consider how important that is to our research questions. If it is important, then is there a place to record shrugs or facial expressions, as some of these could be significant in the analysis of the data.

There is also the consideration of the effect of power differentials on the answers that participants give; for example, if you are the supervisor of a setting and you interview practitioners over the issue of outdoor play, then they might well feel the need to provide answers that they believe you will approve of, so what do you do in that situation? Maybe an interview is not the best tool to choose, as in the case above, anonymity cannot be achieved, and therefore the power differential will always overshadow the data collected. Ingram and Elliott (2020) discuss the differences between individual and small group interviews, and in the scenario above, practitioners might be more likely to be able to answer honestly in a small group interview, whereby the power differential is to the group and not just one individual. Indeed, in a group, practitioners might well feel emboldened to share their view. This might also be true of young children, who will naturally seek to please you if they know you well.

So, if you are planning to use the method of interview as a research tool, use the following checklist to help your data collection.

- Do I have all the necessary permissions?

- Have I arranged a convenient date and time?

- Am I able to minimise distractions?

- How will I record the interview?

- Do I have the questions? Will it be structured with a set collection of questions or semi-structured allowing you to follow up on interesting points?

- How will I record the interview and how will I make sure that the data is securely kept?

With interviews, it is usual practice to transcribe the data so that it is available should a marker wish to see it and so that you can more readily analyse it. How will you do this? Using software that both recognises voice and provides a text version obviously saves a lot of time. Some students have recently recorded their interviews on Microsoft Teams and have had the transcription running alongside. This is time-saving and can allow you to check that you heard correctly.

Questionnaires

Questionnaires lend themselves to being able to collect a large amount of data within a short time frame, but they need to be carefully designed to illicit useful data that has real contextual information as well as research topic-related questions. You need to be sure that the person completing the questionnaire fits the demographic that you have chosen to research. So, for example, if you choose to do an online questionnaire and wish to recruit practitioners working with babies, then you need to establish that these are the people answering your questions. You may need contextual questions so that the participant can declare their context first.

Questionnaires can be designed so that only closed questions are asked, and quantitative analysis can be used, or they might be open-ended requiring a narrative response. Some students choose to have a mixture of questions.

So, if you are planning to use the method of questionnaire as a research tool, use the following checklist to help your data collection:

- Am I clear about who I want to answer the questionnaire?

- Is the questionnaire accessible to my chosen participants?

- Where will I circulate/distribute my questionnaires? If the questionnaire is to be a physical copy in a physical location, then have I gained all the necessary permissions to distribute it?

- How many replies can I handle? Have I made sure that I am clear about cut-off dates or numbers?

- How will I anonymise my data?

There are now many possible routes that student researchers can use for the distribution of questionnaires. If you are intending to use online methods to recruit participants and distribute questionnaires, then you should look at Research

Methods for Education in the Digital Age by Savin-Baden and Tombs (2017), specifically the section on Digital Ethics.

Questionnaires can be given in physical paper form, and this is often the best way if you want to capture data at a specific event (for example, after parent consultations in an early years class). Here your potential participants are 'a captive audience' so to speak, and you can explain your research, gain permission and capture data all at the same time on one physical document. If you are seeking to harness parent voice on any aspect of practice, then it is worth thinking about the times when your potential participants will be easily accessible (and, in theory, have a few minutes to spare) and time your data collection around the setting or school calendar. This obviously needs planning, but it is a golden opportunity for this kind of research.

Questionnaires that are emailed or sent out by another party (for example, the gatekeeper) can fail to generate many responses for the work that has been put into them. This can be disappointing, so if possible, think about how the contact can be more personal.

Data management

Once you have the valuable data, you need to be careful to take care of it. Ingram and Elliott (2020 page 186) remind us that 'clarity is essential in dealing with the labelling of data'. They advise that you think through and set up the system before you actually collect any data so that it can be immediately stored safely ready for the analysis phase. They further remind us about the requirements to act within the data protection laws if you gather data that is not fully anonymous.

The other thing to remember is the pseudonyms that you have given individuals or institutions. If you are collecting a series of data over time, you will need to remember which is setting A, for example. This seems so obvious, but if your research takes place over a period of time, it is so easy to forget which setting is which and this would obviously seriously compromise your research. Keep a note of your key in a secure place.

Ready to go

If you are conducting your research somewhere other than your own setting, then there are a few other considerations to take into account. The first is the exact location of the setting and how long it will take you to get there. It might also be worth enquiring about parking facilities.

Another consideration that has thrown some of our students this year is the dress code. We had negotiated access to a comparative setting for a student, and a week before the student was due to attend, the school, in this instance, sent through a very formal dress code that they expected the student to adhere to. This was unforeseen and meant the student had to find suitable allowable clothes that were very different from those that they wore in their own workplace. You really have to think about everything that might come up, and asking students to enquire about dress codes was a new one to us.

So if visiting a setting that is new to you, have you:

- Made sure you know how to get there and how long the journey takes?
- Enquired about parking/where the bus stops?
- Asked if there is any specific dress code for visitors?
- Checked their CRB requirements?
- Asked for a copy of their safeguarding policy?
- Sent or emailed them all the details of your research (including relevant permissions needed) and arranged an arrival time?
- Checked to make sure that there will be enough time to complete the task.
- Made sure that you have a named contact to ask for when you arrive.
- Do not be surprised if you are asked to hand in your mobile phone on arrival.
- Make sure considering the point above that you have any equipment you need to gather your data.

All of this might seem obvious, but the obvious is only obvious if you have thought about it beforehand. One student I was supervising was visiting a colleague's nursery for the morning to do a peer observation for her research and spent a good ten minutes looking for the doorway into the setting. The door wasn't obvious and she was unaware that the nursery was set within another organisation's building. A further student was visiting a military nursery set within a barracks and was unable to gain access through the barrack's entrance to even get to the nursery as the nursery had not informed the guardsman that they were expecting a visitor. The same was also true for a student who was visiting a social project for prisoner dads and then, having travelled 30 miles, was denied entry as they had no record of him at the front gate. So maybe I need to add another point, and check that entry to your setting isn't obscured or the gift of yet another 'gatekeeper'.

Whilst those students could reflect on the humour of their experience, they wasted a lot of time in having to re-arrange the data collection and this was extremely frustrating for them.

Documents as data

In some methodologies, document collection will feature as one of the methods of data collection. Some documents that you might want to analyse are publicly available. Other documents might be personal such as children's drawings, photographs, assessment data and work samples. The publicly available documents are already freely available, so whilst we would expect respectful use of these, there are not too many ethical issues in using them; however, personal documentary data must be treated with the utmost respect, and some artefacts, such as drawings, etc., should be returned to the participants at the end of the research rather than destroyed.

One student's research question concerned why early years settings are named in the way that they are; for example, names such as Curious Cats, Little Angels and Tumbling Teds, or derivations of these are not uncommon.

So the research question was 'Does a setting's name reflect a specific ethos or is there some other reason for choosing it?' One of the main sources of data for this study was the documents readily available online such as prospectuses or brochures. These were analysed to determine what you could ascertain about the ethos of the setting. The student then sent out questionnaires to the owners of the settings and asked if they would be happy to be interviewed. A few responded and the combination of documentary data and researcher-gathered data produced an interesting study.

The conceptual analysis involved looking at how childhood is constructed in our society and how that impacts the 'marketing' of a brand. What started as one thing developed into a deeper sociological analysis and this is what you have to be prepared for when analysing your data. Through the collection of data, new ideas and areas to investigate will become evident and the project becomes organic. You do, however, need to keep focused on the original question and remember that you will only have ethical clearance for the actions that you specified in your ethical clearance document. If the data makes you doubt your ability to complete the project satisfactorily, then you need to talk to your supervisor and, if necessary, apply to modify your ethical submission to include further methods or actions. For instance, in the above study, the student became really interested in what the parents felt about the names of the settings. The idea of interviewing parents was not part of her original application, but because of the interesting responses from the owners, which tended to centre around marketing strategies, she wanted to see if the name of the setting had had any influence on the parent's choice of setting A over setting B. In turn, she modified the title of her project to 'The influences that are at play in naming an Early Years setting in Southwest England'. As you can see, even through the data collection process, she was constantly refining the study. You have to be able to live with the idea that during the data collection process you might well be surprised with what you are finding and might need to be willing to modify and/or extend your initial ideas in order to refine and provide a deeper, more meaningful conclusion.

Desk-based dissertations/projects

Some research questions will not necessitate the gathering of first-hand data; for example, the question 'Why did the EYFS come about?' can be answered by completing a systematic literature review. In this instance, the student would be expected to carry out a systematic and thorough trawl of all the policy announcements and documents that were produced before the advent of the first iteration of the Early Years Foundation Stage (EYFS). These documents are the data.

So with desk-based research, you need to collect and analyse the existing literature that exists in your study area. This will involve extensive searches of databases to discover the articles, books, policies and reports that have contributed to existing knowledge about the chosen area. You will need to keep detailed notes on what you read and look for consensus, differences and gaps in the information. You will be looking for the common trends and maybe also looking at the chronology of the ideas to see their development over time. You might need to be aware of political ideas at the time the document was written and contextualise the document for the reader. You will then need to draw conclusions, highlight gaps in our understanding and make suggestions for future research or practice that arise from the data that you have presented.

Whatever your chosen methodology is and whatever methods you employ, data collection can be both the most satisfying and the most disrupted part of the research project. The satisfaction comes from discovering new angles and ideas, and the disruption can come from the practicalities and from the discoveries made that might challenge us.

References

Hamilton, L., & Corbett-Whittier, C. (2012). *Using Case Study in Education Research* (1st ed.). SAGE Publications.

Ingram, J., & Elliott, V. (2020). *Research Methods for Classroom Discourse* (3rd ed.). Bloomsbury Academic.

Oates, R., & Hey, C. (2014). *The Student Practitioner in Early Childhood Studies* (3rd ed.). Routledge.

Papatheodorou, T., Luff, P., & Gill, J. (2011). *Child Observation for Learning and Research* (1st ed.). Routledge.

Rogers, S., & Evans, J. (2008). *Inside Role-Play in Early Childhood Education: Researching Young Children's Perspectives* (3rd ed.). Taylor & Francis Group.

Savin-Baden, M., & Tombs, G. (2017). *Research Methods for Education in the Digital Age* (3rd ed.). Bloomsbury.

7 Data analysis
Marie Bradwell

Introduction

This chapter is an overview of things you could do in analysing your data and potential pitfalls to avoid.

Too often (yes, lecturers, researchers and students of all levels of study) waste time stressing over how to analyse data and remain using unworkable techniques or those not suited for the data we have collected. Instead of persevering, the analysis method can be changed and adapted, which of course you should discuss with your supervisor. The emphasis in this chapter will be on how to get the most from your data and how to link it back to your literature review. I also emphasise the need to seek supervision at this time, as this is a crucial moment for advice from a supervisor.

What is research analysis? Why is this important?

So, you have collected your data, whether this is qualitative or quantitative, and transcribed or collated it into a formatted document(s). So now what? Time to draw out the meaning behind and within the data. The analysis quite simply is what is the data telling you? To find out what the data is saying, the data should be inspected, interpreted and sectioned into parts that make sense to you as the researcher.

The separate parts provide topics within the data that you, the researcher, can discuss in sections and link to your literature review. The analysis is essential as this leads into the most extensive section, the most significant chapter(s) of your dissertation or any research project's findings. Some dissertations will have separate chapters on findings and discussion; others will have a chapter where the findings and discussion are presented as one piece. The choice between these being separate or combined links to the discipline that the research sits in, personal preference and listening to advice from your supervisors.

Analysis of the data

So how do we analyse data? We do this systematically by using a technique, an approach and a method of analysis.

The need to adopt a systematic approach cannot be emphasised enough. You don't want to make your job harder by randomly chewing over data without a clear purpose or a system. Howells and Gregory in Austin (2016) consider this as a slow reveal process whereby with each piece of data you analyse, you get clues to the big picture, and the big picture hopefully answers your research question. They liken this to the popular TV gameshow *Catchphrase*, where pieces of a picture that depicts a catchphrase are slowly revealed, and it is the contestant's job to analyse the significance of each small detail to the potential answer.

Clark et al. (2021) state that the research analysis is inextricably linked to the topic, the question and the answers drawn from the data. The choice of technique will depend on the type of data, the overarching question and what you, as the researcher, seek. It is essential to note that your research is unique to you, so do not choose an analysis technique just because your closest peer is using it. The method may not be the right one for your research, and this will lead you into a pitfall – a lack of clarity in understanding and being able to draw out of your data the threads, the sub-topics and the details that go with the research topic and reveal the big picture.

The analysis must not be forced; this is a delicate process that captivates the researcher and the reader when you come to write about the threads in your findings/discussion chapter. You will need time to do this analysis, so make sure that you factor this into your timeline.

Types of Analysis – Qualitative Data. There are several types of analysis that a researcher can choose from. This section sets out what these are and how they relate to specific methods, and how choosing the correct analysis for your question will support the finding of the answers you sought.

Thematic analysis

The thematic analysis technique explores the patterns of meaning within the data (Braun and Clarke 2013). A thematic analysis examines similarities, experiences, opinions, or views within and across groups. For instance, the data can be text, voices or pictures of the participants. Braun and Clarke (2006) state that the themes come from the significance of the research question. However, the explorations and themes may lead to the research questions being adapted or further questions being raised, and then the data will require revisiting. A drawback of this type of analysis is that it is time-consuming.

Grounded analysis

In grounded analysis, one case study is the start of the process. A theory can begin to be formulated from reading through and exploring the case study. From this point onwards, draw in other case studies to be reviewed and analysed, and the developed theory can be tested. By extending the case study collection, the formula for the new approach can be amended and adapted as required. Often, grounded theory is used where there is little existing knowledge of a topic. The systematic procedure for grounded theory analysis is observed as reading the data, coding the data and repeating the process until saturation is reached (Bryman, 2015). The data is then compared and contrasted.

Content analysis

The content analysis method is used when the researcher looks for frequencies in the text. When categorising the data, the regularity of the words or phrases used is coded. In addition, the frequency of a shared idea can be included or specified as meaningful. Large amounts of text for coding can be a barrier for using this analysis technique, as this is time-consuming. In addition, the meaning in or behind the text can be lost somewhat with this technique.

Narrative analysis

The analysis of a narrative approach involves exploring the stories being told by the individual. Eames et al. (2016) specify that the narrative approach values people as experts in their own lives. The narrative system incorporates how the stories are told, thinking and acknowledging the emotion, the diction and the mood. The narrative analysis provides awareness of people's perspectives (Andrews et al., 2013). Within this type of study analysis, participant numbers are usually small due to the time-consuming aspects of collecting and then analysing the data.

Discourse analysis

An approach that focuses on language and debate, explored through a social or cultural context. The group dynamics of understanding the conversation are analysed. How people converse about topics in these social or cultural contexts is observed and analysed. The conversations can be followed on a one-to-one basis or in a group circumstance. The history, either the social past or the cultural account, is relevant here. The past is of importance due to the present context of the discussion. The power within these conversations is also often observed; the balance of power in conversation is equal or unequal and can be analysed. The emphasis on the topic must be exact to truly analyse the data. Again, the point of saturation is relevant in this technique of analysis.

Interpretative phenomenological analysis

The interpretative phenomenological analysis (IPA) analysis is used when exploring a significant life event. The experience of which is for individuals largely interpretive. The knowledge of the incident that occurred is discussed. The analysis is less about the subject and its commonalities. Instead, the focus is on the relevance for the individual. The researcher must have self-awareness when using this analysis if they have experienced the event they are researching.

Quantitative data

Whilst quantitative data is easier to handle and display, the analysis is still of utmost importance.

Quantitative data is often best displayed in charts and graphs. These are then, if left without an explanation, open to interpretation, so you need to contextualise the data and explain your analysis of what the chart or graph shows.

So firstly, when you start to construct your chart or graph, make sure that you choose (see Table 7.1) the most appropriate format for your data. This will depend upon the nature of the data and what it is that you want to show. For example, if you wanted to show that the majority of respondents supported one viewpoint, then a pie chart might be the best way to make that point, as visually you can see the proportions of 'the pie'.

If you are using any chart or graph, you must remember to label the axis or the portion so that the chart makes sense to the reader.

There also needs to be an appropriate scale so that the information is not distorted due to the scale of the graph.

Colour and formatting decisions also help to draw attention to key points. Context for any information is key, as is the clarity of the chart/graph. Do not overclutter the page where the graph or chart is. The information should be able to be viewed clearly.

Table 7.1

The Analysis Method	The Research Focus
Discourse	Language: conversations, meaning in a cultural or social context
Content	The words: what words are used, how are these used, the frequency of terms used
Thematic	Experiences, opinions. The similarities and uniqueness of these
IPA	Events: the experience of the same event, told by various individuals
Narrative	Stories: exploring the stories of people
Grounded theory	Developing: a new theory or revising a theory

Choosing a suitable analysis method – what is your research focus? What is your question trying to find out?

The topic, the question, the methodology and the methods will determine the analysis. For instance, if your question seeks to explore childbirth experiences from a father's perspective, you could use IPA to analyse. If you are examining the conversations between midwives and parents in English culture, the analysis would be discourse. The content analysis of the question sets would be used to observe, for instance, the frequency of set terms used in developmental exams of preschool children. The narrative analysis would ask for the parents' story about choosing a preschool for their child, whereas the thematic analysis may seek to explore children's opinions about their setting. If you desire to refute an existing theory or develop a new one, then grounded analysis is the technique for you to choose.

Familiarity with the data, interpreting and drawing conclusions

Go with your gut-what feels right, don't be afraid to change – even if this means altering your ethics with your supervisors. Getting the most from your data requires colour coding, either manually or using a program.

Thinking about authenticity and trustworthiness

Within qualitative research and the analysis process, researchers are called to ensure there is an underpinning of authenticity and trustworthiness. Guba and Lincoln (2005) specify there are four threads within this: credibility, transferability, confirmability and dependability. An example of how theming or coding data might be is given in Table 7.2.

Table 7.2 Example chart of theming data

Data	Subthemes	Themes
House points equal play, likes activities that are not formally academic	Curriculum and differentiation	Curriculum
Enjoys things that are different to that which peers are interacting with	Relationships – siblings	Relationships
Important things in life are food, ICT and knowing where his brothers are	Practitioners	Practitioners
Enjoys forest school – it's 'wonderful'	**Self-awareness**	**Self**
TAs that play and listen are identified. Jaime identified different school adults to support him in other areas of need. **Hunger, tiredness and emotions**	**Own needs** and identification of who meets these	Practitioners
Also identified the admin lady as she collects dinner orders **when people arrive late to school**		Practitioners

Here the student was researching relationships in that are important to children transitioning to the Reception Class.

Credibility is supported by transparency

Within the research process, transparency is evidenced through the provision of information, informed consent and withdrawal, available and acknowledged by the participants (Hammersley and Traianou, 2012). This links to the choice of methods, which must be a consistent and rational match for the research question (Bardach 2015). Furthermore, participants' experiences and knowledge are required to be relevant to the research question (Bryman, 2015). It is of importance for researchers to always maintain openness and honesty about the research with participants. Enabling transparency through these processes provides transferability across research to be repeated and extended (Guba and Lincoln, 2015, Maxwell, 2013).

Trustworthiness is supported by upholding participants' voice retaining its validity

An avenue for preserving this is via discussion of results with participants (Crotty, 1998). Mack (2010) discusses that, within qualitative research, there is a pathway for multiple truths. Therefore, discussion and acknowledgement of participants' views are imperative. This author has stayed faithful to the data, respecting the voice of each participant.

Surviving and thriving

Different university establishments run the dissertation or project module in various ways: some with face-to-face lectures, others with supervisory support and some offer a mixture of the two. Regardless of which way or how your institution supports the dissertation process, you will have a supervisor. At this stage of your dissertation, it is imperative that you be in regular contact with your supervisor. Hopefully, by this point, you will have built a two-way communication relationship with your supervisor. This will help during the analysis and write-up process. The analysis, as we have seen in this chapter, is not always a clear-cut or simple procedure. It relies on your interpretation, knowledge of the overall subject matter and the question you are asking, confidence and a little bit of confusion thrown in. Confusion is part and parcel of the analysis process and can be embraced, even when this feels uncomfortable; this is when you need those conversations with your supervisor. Your supervisor is there to talk through the confusion with you, discuss the topics and the themes that come from dissecting the data and even to take the journey with you to support you in finding those themes. Do not leave it to chance that your supervisor will be available at the drop of a hat; plan in advance for those lengthy conversations. BUT remember, supervisors are readily available at the end of an email; it is always better to email than to sit and wander if you should or shouldn't.

References

Andrews, M. Squire, C., & Tamboukou, M. (2013). *Doing Narrative Research* (2nd ed.) London: Sage.

Austin, R. (2016). *Researching Primary Education* (3rd ed.). Sage.

Bardach, E. (2015). *A Practical Guide for Policy Analysis the Eightfold Path to More Effective Problem Solving* (4th ed.). Sage.

Braun, V., & Clarke, V. (2006). Using Thematic Analysis in Psychology. *Qualitative Research in Psychology*, *3*(2), 77–101. https://doi.org/10.1191/1478088706qp063oa.

Braun, V., & Clarke, V.. (2013) *Successful Qualitative Research a Practical Guide for Beginners*, London: Sage.

Bryman, A. (2015). *Social Research Methods* (5th ed.). Sage.

Clark, T., Foster, L., Sloan, L., & Bryman, A.. (2021) *Bryman's Social Research Methods* (6th ed.) Oxford: Oxford University Press.

Crotty, M. (1998). *The Foundations of Social Research* (3rd ed.). Sage.

Eames, V., Shippen, C., & Sharp, H. (2016). The Team of Life: A Narrative Approach to Building Resilience in UK School Children. *Educational and Child Psychology*, *33*(2), 57–68.

Guba, E. G., & Lincoln, Y. S. (2005). Paradigmatic Controversies, Contradictions, and Emerging Confluences. In N. K. Denzin & Y. S. Lincoln (Eds.), *The Sage Handbook of Qualitative Research* (pp. 191–215). Sage Publications Ltd.

Guba, E., Lincoln, Y., & Lynham, S. (2018). Paradigmatic Controversies, Contradictions and Emerging Confluences Revisited. In N. Denzin & Y. Lincoln (Eds.), *The Sage Handbook of Qualitative Research* (5th ed., pp. 108–150). Sage.

Hammersley, M., & Traianou, A. (2012). *Ethics in Qualitative Research: Controversies and Contexts*. Sage.

Hammersley, M. (2013). Using Visual Data in Research on Childhood. In *Childhoods in Context* (2nd ed., pp. 263–297). Policy Press.

Kinnunen, S., & Einarsdottir, J. (2013). Feeling, Wondering, Sharing and Constructing Life: Aesthetic Experience and Life Changes in Young Children's Drawing Stories. *International Journal of Early Childhood*, *45*(3), 359–385. https://doi.org/10.1007/s13158-013-0085-2

Mack, L. (2010). The Philosophical Underpinnings of Educational Research. *Polyglossia*, *19*, 5–11. https://secure.apu.ac.jp/rcaps/uploads/fckeditor/publications/polyglossia/Polyglossia_V19_Lindsay.pdf

Maxwell, J. A. (2013). *Qualitative Research Design: An Interactive Approach*. Applied Social Research Methods Series (3rd ed.). Sage.

Shenton, A. K. (2004). Strategies for Ensuring Trustworthiness in Qualitative Research Projects. *Education for Information*, *22*(2), 63–75. https://doi.org/10.3233/EFI-2004-22201

8 Recommendations and conclusions

Alison Milner

Recommendations and conclusions are important in many ways as they acknowledge your reflection on the study that you have carried out. This chapter focuses on how to present your outcomes, acknowledging problems encountered and how you make realistic justifications for the importance of your study to others. Often when engaging in research, there is a misperception that all output (how you tell people about your findings and conclusions) should be academic. This chapter seeks to guide you through the many ways output can be managed in a more practical, often useful way to support the impact of your findings.

As with all research, there are many aspects of the process that appear important at given times throughout the journey. One of the most important aspects of research, however, is the dissemination or output of shared findings. Why may you ask is this important? Well, the fact remains that if you do research and never share the output, then the point or value of the research could be lost. As such, the loss of knowledge from the research could mean that the impact of your findings on others: professionals, practitioners and teachers may not benefit from your insight, to inform or change practice. Whilst there are many ways to explore the myriad outputs of research, how you decide to showcase your findings is all part of the research journey.

This chapter explores the different terms of reference related to the action of dissemination, identifying the various ways the different approaches may work for you and your research project. Firstly, I will begin by discussing some key terms, including output, impact and dissemination. Smith and Walker (2022) discuss the various ways dissemination can form formal outputs from research projects, suggesting that, in some cases, the output of the research can, in part, depend on the person sharing the research and/or the community of practice receiving the findings. As with all research, the dissemination of the data is as dependent on the audience receiving the output as the chosen design. Remembering that the process of dissemination/output does not need to be formal, it can be as simple as sharing your findings in a conversation or sharing good practice.

Output – what does this mean?

We will begin by exploring the term output. What does this mean in research terms? Well, output is the information generated from the result of conducting research. Research endeavours require a set of protocols or processes to be followed, with careful consideration prior to the output of the research. How this is shared and how this looks depend on the researcher and or the purpose of the study. Ritchie and Spencer (1994) and Smith and Firth (2011) assert that output can often be descriptive, or a summary of the semantic meanings resultant from the data, while at the same time leading to actionable accessibility for practitioners and those with a vested interest in the project (Braun and Clarke, 2021). Therefore, trying to maintain a pragmatic approach to ensure the output is relatable to the audience assures the impact of the research. In turn, consideration of output accessibility guarantees that, where appropriate, participants' voices are heard as a valued contribution to change/s in professional practice. Rememb that the participants' input generates an output relevant to, and for the development of, the wider professional arena.

Impact – what does this mean and how can I get involved?

Impact, or the term impact, in research terminology perhaps conjures visions of a meaningful engagement in academic scholarship. This, however, is not necessarily the case. Impact denotes the potential influence or strong significance that transpires from the research findings. The impact or influence of research on knowledge acquisition or practice remains aligned to the researcher or practices' relevance to the study. Also, the impact of the research can alter or change practice, thought patterns and attitudes on an individual level. Therefore, the impact of the research, though still significant, can be far more meaningful to the individuals or audience than the original intentions of the output – as an academic contribution to a journal or publication.

Practitioner research, therefore, does not need to be caught up in the academic processes adopted for the assessment of projects. Moreover, research can be a straightforward study conducted to improve a template, process or recording a child's progress in their learning. The whole idea of research is linked to the requirement to place some time and space aside to think, pragmatically, about a problem that you would like to solve (Action research, Lewin, 1946), or to develop a better understanding about practices that are working very well (Appreciative Inquiry, Cooperrider & Srivastva, 1987). In this way, impactful research makes a difference in some way, to practice, and individuals involved in learning and education.

To ensure the impact, output and dissemination of the research is 'fit for purpose' you may wish to consider the research design; checking that how you are going to conduct the research is in tune with your choice of output. This is probably the best way to approach research to understand how or why you are doing the research, and then connecting the two for the best output for your needs. Developing a series of questions or protocols for your research has been discussed in the previous chapters, outlining the research process. As with any research project, the set requirements begin with consideration of the research area to be studied. Once identified, the next step is to outline how the data will initially be gathered, to answer the question posed. Earmarking the sample group, where and with whom the data will be collected again, signifies a thoughtful approach to the study. All these areas of the research are incorporated into the ethics process to ensure that you and your participants are safe during and after the research has been conducted. As such, the output of the research project should fulfil the ethical requirements, guaranteeing that participants' information is safe.

Dissemination – how do I best showcase my findings?

Dissemination of research can be divided into three sections: the method, transfer of information and transfer of knowledge (National Children's Bureau (NCB), 2017). Each of the three sections provides a useful connection and understanding between the chosen activities for optimum researcher engagement. The first involves the researcher sharing findings in the form of best practice; this type of information sharing can come from policymakers to support new or evolving practices in education. Drawing on previous research from articles or practice from knowledgeable others (Vygotsky, 1962), we can begin to share knowledge more openly. These initiatives, whilst useful, are aimed at providing a rough guide to enhance practice in the classroom, management and/or for the development of strategies to support teaching and learning. Changes documented in practice are often ignored as being part of normalised expectations. However, with the inclusion of evidence-informed practice supporting research, the value of the amendments or changes introduced by practitioners in their pedagogy supports dissemination. It is at this point that the inclusion of training either within settings or at workshops held within conferences or not can also be included as a form of formal dissemination from research findings.

Whilst these approaches are not limited to educational settings, the formal reporting often shared in this form of dissemination tends to be more directive. Regularly, this may be the nature of your own research, where the findings would enhance and improve performativity in the classroom leading to dissemination in this form. However, as it often the case with practitioner research or projects at undergraduate level, the output is related to action in practice. As McNiff (2013) suggests, action research can be completed and disseminated by practitioners for practitioners. Therefore, the very idea of dissemination, whilst formal in some parts, can and does impact the general day-to-day professional practice, working in educational settings.

How do I showcase the voices of my participants?

As has been discussed earlier in this chapter, the value of dissemination should not be an afterthought. It should in many ways be at the forefront of the research decision-making process. Ultimately, whatever you choose to research should contribute to new knowledge being explored, as has previously been discussed, or to instigate a change in practice. Whether you research dissemination approach is to herald the evidence for change, then the communication beyond the research should be clear for the audience it is intended. Questions, such as if or how interactive the research output is going to be, and or any involvement with professional development, become more pressing as the conceptualised dissemination approach considers the planning stage of the research design. The transformative stage of the research design is the shared output, either to other outside of the project itself or with the participants who have contributed to the study. Being a part of the transformation of practice, whether small or large, can have a motivational aspect for the community of practice (Wenger, 1998), supporting the agency of those involved.

How do I showcase change in/for practice?

Conferences/events (interactive) others, where good practice cascades down from the top.

Knowledge transfer?

Networking (active participants). As the word spreads, the practice is adopted at each level by the whole community of teachers.

Highlighting the need for further research, you will be pleased to know that you are not expected to carry out further studies, you are just indicating that this is what you know needs to be addressed to further explore your research question. This is a true critical reflection of what you have learned about your topic and how far you have been able to answer your original research questions.

The many practical ways to disseminate findings: the how and why of dissemination for impact in practice

Informal ways

A few informal ways will be discussed as appropriate ways to document how you will inevitably share your findings or output with an audience. These informal approaches are generally conducted through conversations. Remembering that often the important messages or anecdotes are shared by 'more knowledgeable others' (Vygotsky, 1962), whether these pearls of wisdom are shared by leaders in practice or colleagues who have been practicing for several years. You must not forget that if you have engaged in research, you also have knowledge to share from your experiences that have been generated from evidence-informed practices. Firstly, conversations with colleagues are a unique, yet poignant way of sharing your thoughts or ideas generated from research output. The value of shared adaptations over a Cuppa can be less threatening, leading to an equality in the sharing, that on a level can be just as meaningful as the information of research output gained from reading an academic article. Often with informal conversations with colleagues, the formal academic language has been converted into plain speaking language that has value and meaning in the context of practice-based pedagogical inquiry. The networking, inwardly or outwardly, of your research supports connectivity between colleague and or peers, again reinforcing the benefits of knowledge sharing.

Likewise, the informal conversations with parents of children within your settings can also convey a valuable message. Again, the nature of sharing output from research in this way removes the formality of telling someone about your findings to a natural conversation shared in a comfortable manner about ways to improve practices, such as how to instigate changes in behaviour between the children and parents in a situation or scenario. Often, parents rely on the experience and advice shared by practitioners. Practitioners experience many different interactions daily and are often well placed to share their knowledgeable thoughts with parents, as required. Even when you perceive conversations to be of no consequence, it is important to remember the value of your words when you are sharing your experience or research with parents. Parents can come to rely on the wealth of experience shared by practitioners when they are trying to potty train or encourage their children to sleep through the night.

Lastly, conversations with children are an important way to disseminate the findings of your research, either if it is linked to a formal research project as part of a qualification or even if the output of your research is aligned to the informal research conducted in the workplace. Both are important mechanisms to generate change/s in practice, behaviours or processes for all involved in education. Each of the suggestions for informal dissemination could be adopted to ensure that your research is shared with the right audience. Nevertheless, deciding who and how your research should be disseminated can be discussed with supervisors or the leadership team to guarantee you are pitching your research in in the best way possible. Remember, many research projects often remain unread or discarded once they are committed to paper. If you fear your research will go unnoticed or changes and amendments linked to your findings become ignored, maybe share your findings with colleagues, parents of the children you engage with on a daily basis and/or not forgetting the children, if related, when presented appropriately, may be interested too. If you are choosing to disseminate your research with children, this is also a wonderful opportunity for you to think about the language you are using to share your results.

Activity

Consider the various ways you can disseminate your research. Try speaking to your reflection for three minutes about your research; for an added challenge,

imagine your audience are colleagues, parents or children (alternatively, try all three at different intervals to understand the nuanced adaptations depending on the audience). Reflect on the way you adapt your language to ensure your message is shared effectively. Note the key words you use, how can they be interpreted and could you adopt some of the terminology for formal dissemination?

Think carefully about the nature of your message, what do you want to convey from your research. At this point, it may be a good idea to try the aforementioned activity – attempting to condense your research into a three-minute verbal self-contained disseminated presentation. From this activity, you will begin to identify the individual messages from your research that you feel would be worthwhile sharing. Beyond this activity, if you are still unsure what the messages are, then you could ask your setting, colleagues or, in the case of you being engaged in academic study, your tutors. Once you have decided on the best approach to take to disseminate your research, you can begin to refine your message with consideration of your audience, language and supportive literature to enhance your output.

Formal dissemination options

Formal ways of dissemination can be used in several different ways to improve and inform the practice of fellow professionals. These formal approaches can include staff meetings, internal or external training sessions and posters, either for sharing within the organisation or in a more formal academic forum. The formal dissemination of research can also be in the form of publication to an academic journal or on occasion within the industry, for example, in the early years educator or other early years or educational publications.

Staff meetings are a great way to disseminate your research with colleagues. Depending on the regularity or your meetings, the opportunity to share your findings with colleagues, although often a daunting prospect, peer feedback or comments can appear a bit scary at the beginning, but I speak from experience, peers often welcome thoughts and evidence-informed comments connected to the development and/or improvement of practice, so have a go! The great part about sharing your research in staff meetings is that it can lead to an in-depth discussion around your findings, adaptations and developments for future practice. These occasions also may lead to shedding light on an area of practice that has previously been ignored or that colleagues may have also been struggling with in their practice/classroom pedagogy. Remember you bring a unique approach to your research that places you in a privileged position of knowledgeable. However, do not forget that you are always learning and can gain from the shared experience to further develop your pedagogical practices, big or small.

Training sessions

The activity of sharing good practice or research findings has become synonymous with the evolving nature of educational development for practitioners. Introducing new ways to conduct practice or new procedures can often be supported by evidence-informed research, especially when organised to develop and improve practice/s. The output of your research has the potential to generate training materials supporting the dissemination of new information, to be cascaded out to colleagues old and new. Training sessions, either internal to the organisation or for a wider audience, are a useful way to share new information learnt or acquired from research. The community created when new processes are shared sometimes generates unique insight for/in the preparation of innovative approaches for adoption into practice. Not only does the community surrounding the information in the form of a training session or series of sessions draw people together, but it also ensures a shared experience. Whether the experience is good or bad, sharing research findings in this way can produce discussions beyond the initial dissemination, further unifying individuals who are in attendance. The value of disseminating information in this forum outwardly benefits both the researcher and those in receipt of the output. Discussion supports the continuous improvement of practices in a shared space between colleagues, to feel empowered and motivated in their roles. These shared spaces do not need individuals to be physically present. Virtual environments are becoming a popular alternative to physical communities, making knowledge sharing much more accessible to many more people.

Since the electronic advancements of technology experienced during the global lockdowns, the number of online trainings has escalated. Innovatively reaching many more professionals in the educational community, online trainings are now available globally, ensuring there are always colleagues and fellow researchers willing to listen to research output. Increasingly, the global information transfer resulting from online forums does establish a greater comparative element to research output in the transferability of practice worldwide. When considered in light of the changes that have taken place in recent years, the opportunity to engage in online training is increasing the accessibility of your own research to reach further afield. Although classed as a formal mechanism of output, online training sessions are certainly more cost-effective, reducing the travel costs of attending sessions whilst drawing practitioners together from communities in many different countries.

Conference presentations

Conferences are often considered a congregation of academic individuals far removed from the average practitioner in early years or school settings. However, increasingly, there are opportunities for practitioners from all pedagogical disciplines to engage in the sharing of research informed practice/s at conferences. The forum generated at these events create spaces to commune and discuss the findings of research, from all stages of the research journey. I, myself, during the early stages of my research, attended several conferences, presenting my research progress at that given time; not only were these occasions and opportunity for me to share my intentions, but they were also a welcome chance to receive feedback from likeminded individuals with research experience. It is important to remember research output is not necessarily the formation of a concluded research project. Research output can be from any stage of the research that you consider has significance for practice, and/or practitioners to gain from the experience of your research at that time.

The accessibility of conference attendance has also altered over the last few years, in part due to the global lockdowns. Online conferences, undoubtedly, create a different atmosphere but, even so, they are a useful way to tap into many different areas of practice in one event. However, there is still a place for in person conferences with moderated sessions fielding any questions posed by the audience and keeping the speaker to timings. A medium to promote your findings, to disseminate conclusions derived from your research journey with additional exploration of a sharing/evaluative environment.

Poster presentations

Posters, research or otherwise, are another visual representation to share your output. Although the content of your poster may depend on the audience reading your findings, there is no denying the value of summarising research in this way. Posters can be a useful medium to communicate a variety of points identified from your research design, supportive literature and ultimately the outcomes of your research. When combined with infographics and pictures to symbolise the visual benefits of the poster, the snapshot disseminated in this condensed medium presents just the right information about your research. The poster enables you to share the literature you value for incorporation into your research, signposting colleagues and fellow researchers about influences you have identified as significant.

Whilst posters can direct the research process in an academic form, they are a useful artefact for conferences, especially when early researchers are initially engaging in academic representation of their findings. Together with conference attendance, posters can be a useful method to generate discussion in small groups or on a one-to-one basis, making them a medium of output, which lends itself to being both aimed at small and larger audiences. There are occasions when posters are shared as part of an extension to the main presentation sessions at a conference, requiring little or no input from a physical presence, during the event itself. Again, this is a possible output for early researchers to dip their toe into the academic world of research dissemination beyond the experience from their academic course of study. Increasingly, posters and poster presentations are incorporated into academic modes of assessment to determine knowledge with condensed information being shared with an audience. It is important to remember posters are a visual representation of your research and, as such, should be treated with carefully considered content. You are not required to share the content of your whole research project.

Activity

Consider the benefits of sharing your research in a short three-minute podcast or interview. This activity can greatly benefit your understanding of your own

output, identifying what is important to share with others, whilst also determining how your output could be disseminated in a different format.

Posters in the workplace are a creative way to share the main points of your research, which can benefit either colleagues, parents and children. Remember, the importance of the poster is to understand your audience, adjusting the content accordingly to maximise their attention and 'takeaways' from your findings. If the poster contains too much information, the likelihood is that the audience will not be able to retain the information. This can lead to the audience finding the poster difficult to interpret and make a meaningful connection with their practice. Workplace posters can be a useful addition for sharing information and can be used to direct changes in processes. As with all evidence-informed research, the aim is to develop and improve practices to benefit holistic child-centred education.

Magazine publications

Practitioner research can often be the most informed research, generated from like-minded colleagues. The shared output from the research findings can stimulate a connection with the experiential benefits of in-depth analysis and evaluation. Therefore, it is useful to consider who and where your disseminated research can be of the most benefit. Due to the time commitment practitioners give to their role, there are often limited opportunities to engage or read materials that require a great deal of focus to interpret academic sourced information. Instead, practitioner-focused research can be most beneficial when it is shared in magazine articles or non-academic journals. If you decide to adopt this approach for your research output, you may find there is more uptake from fellow practitioners for networking opportunities. You may also find that your research findings will be more readily available to read, therefore making a direct difference to practitioners in their settings. The plethora of practitioner-focused publications can be a suitable option for early researcher output. However, deciding which one is best for you can also be a confusing process. This is where communication, regular contact within your setting or attending practitioner-focused events can improve your and others' knowledge about the various methods of outputs for your research.

Links to methods of data collection

As previously mentioned in an earlier section in this chapter, the nature of your research design can significantly direct the type or options for output from your study. As such, consider the unique messages that you are relaying in the research, who is likely to benefit from the messages in your research. Who has been involved in the research? Would those individuals benefit from hearing or being involved in the output from your research? There are a few options to consider: if these questions are linked to your research design, whether you have been engaged in an ethnographic paradigmatic approach or not and how can you best showcase your findings.

The formalisation of ethnographic research embedded with the participants is becoming a popular approach to amplify their voices. The mosaic approach (Clark and Moss, 2011) enables participants to have ownership of the research. Decisions can be made about the methods used combined with the research analysis to co-construct the meanings shared from the findings. This research approach, in some cases, can also be used as a way for children to research their own perceptions of a particular area of focus. There are many ways to use the mosaic approach in research with children. One way would be to introduce or use photographs to promote a visual representation of a child's view of the research, whilst also showcasing a form of dissemination at the same time. The mosaic approach (Clarke and Moss, 2011) does enable the incorporation of a creative medium to be introduced to capture individual perspective and view, without the intervention of researcher bias. Obviously, this does depend on the research design, but it should be considered if you wish to gain insight from the participants' voice. Whilst this might not be an option for your research project, certainly consider what, who and how you are going to engage with the participants and output of your study.

There are always alternatives to disseminate research. The following case studies share two such approaches that have been adopted to share the output. Both of these case studies have enabled engagement with and for the requirement of different audiences; in one case, this was not a planned outcome but became a pivotal aspect of the research dissemination.

CASE STUDY: Using Bead Collage – Alison Milner

For my PhD research, I decided to take a creative methodological approach. This choice enabled me to realise a research design that fulfilled a creative vision with an opportunity to embrace my own positionality in the design of my research tool – bead collage. After reading several articles related to this relatively new approach to research, I could justify the creative methodology. The combination of identity research with bead collage draws on feminist ideals to be informed in a reflective interpretative approach. Consideration of the participants' engagement with their own retelling of academic identity further reinforced the benefits of using bead collage. Again, connecting with the movement of self-identification and change, the process of reflexivity, uncovering the often-hidden thoughts, beliefs and feelings can be realised by the individual. The benefits of combining the use of collage and bead collage support the potential transformation of consciousness to reinterpret new meaning and understanding of self.

The bead collage activity involved participants creating a bead collage, choosing beads from a selection of different sizes, colours and shapes. Each participant could decide how they wished to represent their bead collage, identifying how to frame their completed display. All bead collages would remain unstuck for two reasons: the first, to ensure the beads could be reused for subsequent focus groups, and, second, the participants could make amendments to their final bead collage as they felt they needed to make changes before they had fully finished. The final bead collages could then be either threaded onto a variety of different threads such as silk, laces, ribbon and string or the finished bead collage could be mounted on different coloured cards or papers provided. Despite the many options for mounting the beads, the rationale was to create a moment in time, to remove the pressure to create a static frieze. Instead, the collage could be added to, or adjusted, if the participants felt they needed to from the discussion with others in the group.

The completed collages stimulated individual perspectives with a smorgasbord of unique creative insight, limited only by the participant's imagination. The traditional understanding of collage is aligned with the artistic medium to interpret and explore individual beliefs and ideas. Imitating the interpretative aspect of collage, individual bead collage creations can also replicate personal patterns and symbol representations, depending on the choice of beads included by the participants.

The use of bead collage as a standalone activity has become a mechanism to instil self-reflection, stimulating individuals to pause their daily lives to sit and contemplate how they perceive themselves whilst also representing their interpretations through bead collage. Prior to commencing my research design, I had not foreseen the benefits of transferability of my research tool. It was only later, once I had completed the initial focus groups in my research data collection, that the value of bead collage creation for the purpose of self-reflection was identified.

Now, as I edge closer to the completion of my PhD, I recognise the importance of the research journey I have undertaken. The experience presented various unforeseen opportunities along the way to maximise on the research design. This included the transference of the output generated from my research, combined with requirements to fulfil the academic write-up of the thesis; the real benefit has been the bead collage. As with all research, the importance of the messages sought, or the messages believed to be worth sharing from the outset often, and very much so in my case, alter beyond reason. Adaptation within research is the key to understanding the pathway to be taken. Each individual step of the way insightful events create change in yourself eventually determines the alternative perspective to be considered on the research journey. Dissemination is the ultimate message left behind once the experience of stress and pressure has long gone, after the research deadlines for submission have been fulfilled.

CASE STUDY By Patrick Owens – Film

When planning my dissertation, I imagined a huge 10,000-word document with hours of onerous typing ahead of me. I foresaw long painful evenings of reading and writing whilst propping my head up with academic books. It was only when I proposed my idea of an investigation into the successes of a trauma-informed multi-academy trust, did I discover how creative I could be. My ambitious project supervisor (Jan Gourd) instilled some of her ambition in me and suggested a documentary.

> I took to this and really allowed myself to think freely, considering all my possible options of how I would go about obtaining data, where I would gather this data from, how I could analyse this, what narrative I was creating alongside this and how it was supporting my argument that trauma-informed practice really does work.
>
> One task that followed each step of this project was simplifying and streamlining. Sometimes, ambitions can come with complications, and although I wanted to produce an Attenborough-standard film, I had to consider my timeframe and expenses. After slimming down to the realistic possibilities, I decided to interview staff on their views of the trauma-informed approach in practice. I had considered interviewing children, but this suggested a number of barriers, such as understanding and explaining an abstract concept, prompting without compromising the integrity of the study and obtaining lawful permissions and consent.
>
> This method of gathering quantitative data through interviews proved useful, as not only was I able to gather in-depth opinions and lived experiences, but these responses were open for partial interpretation, which supported my theory. Furthermore, by interviewing those at varying levels of the school hierarchy, I was able to uncover a range of perspectives from strategic to consequential to day-to-day use and running of this approach. This investigative approach provided me with a clear overview of how this worked from top to bottom and, with consistency, worked at all levels too.
>
> Something I did not expect to encounter along the way was how in-depth my legal knowledge around media, recording and consent would need to become, or how long script development would take. I was keen to ensure that I was following all the rules around consent, ethics and legislation, so that all participants were treated equally, and were aware they had autonomy over what was being recorded and how it was later used. In terms of script development, I had two parts to consider: 1. What questions was I asking participants and how can I make them as open as possible? 2. What do my voice-overs need to convey, what are the key messages and themes and how do I want the audience to respond to what they are hearing?
>
> In order to manage this, I used family members as screen-testers, and used their feedback to change and edit the documentary so that the audio-visual experience was pleasing but informative.
>
> My final thought in the planning process was 'who am I targeting with this film?' It was clear to me that this would be a piece angled at professionals, those who needed convincing of the success of, or those who needed educating about this approach. Deciding on this audience allowed me to freely use sector jargon and be comfortable that my audience understood me.

Both case studies illustrate the novel ways dissemination of your research can be approached. Whether there is a formal planned structure to your research output or not, there are many avenues that you can take to engage with your audience beyond the completion of your research gathering stage. As with both the case studies, the value of interaction with your audience impacts the message that you are conveying from your research. Nevertheless, consideration of how you decide to showcase your output is about as much about you as a researcher as it is about the research design. Seek guidance from your supervisors to decide on the best approach to take for the output of your research. If this is not an option, read about how other researchers in your field of experience have disseminated their findings. Alternatively, consider discussions with your colleagues and other practitioners about the best approach to take that would have the most impact with your practice.

This chapter has outlined the various approaches you can take to disseminate your research findings. The contribution that you make as a researcher in your field of expertise should not prevent you from communicating the value of your findings to others. Remember, the output adopt will support the knowledge base within your community of practice. Therefore, choosing the most impactful dissemination for your research supports the way you and your research are seen by other practitioners and researchers. Good luck!

References

Braun, V. and Clarke, V. (2021). *Thematic Analysis: A Practical Guide* [eBook version]. SAGE.

Clark, A., & Moss, P. (2011). Listening to Young Children: The Mosaic Approach (Second edition.). National Children's Bureau.

Cooperrider, D. L., & Srivastva, S. (1987). Appreciative inquiry in organizational life. In: Woodman, R.W., & Pasmore, W.A. (Eds.) *Research in Organizational Change and Development* (pp. 129–169). JAI Press.

Lewin, K. (1946). Action Research and Minority Problems. *Journal of Social Issues*, 2(4), 34–46.

McNiff, J. (Ed.) (2013). *Value and Virtue in Practice-Based Research* (3rd ed.). September Books.

National Children's Bureau (NCB) (2017). *Dissemination of Best Practice in Teaching and Learning Research*. 61 Dissemination-of-Best-Practice-in-Teaching-and-Learning-Research (education-ni.gov.uk). How to disseminate your research | NIHR

Ritchie, J., & Spencer, L. (1994). Qualitative Data Analysis for Applied Policy Research. In: Bryman, A., & Burgess, B. (Eds.) *Analyzing Qualitative Data*. Routledge. http://dx.doi.org/10.4324/9780203413081_chapter_9

Ross-Hellauer, T., Tennant, J. P., Banelytė, V., Gorogh, E., Luzi, D., & Kraker, P., Pisacane, L., Ruggieri, R., Sifacaki, E. and Vignoli, M. (2020). Ten Simple Rules for Innovative Dissemination of Research. *PLOS Computational Biology*, 16(4), e1007704. https://doi.org/10.1371/journal.pcbi.1007704.

Southwell, D., Gannaway, D., Orrell, J., Chalmers, D., & Abraham, C. (2010). Strategies for effective dissemination of the outcomes of teaching and learning projects. *Journal of Higher Education Policy and Management*, 32(1), 55–67.

Smith, J., & Firth, J. (2011). *Qualitative data analysis: The framework approach*. Nurse Researcher, 18(2), 52–62. ISSN 1351-5578

Smith, S., & Walker, D. (2022). Scholarship and teaching-focused roles: An exploratory study of academics' experiences and perceptions of support. *Innovations in Education and Teaching International*, 1–12. https://doi.org/10.1080/14703297.2022.2132981

Southwell, D., Gannaway, D., Orrell, J., Chalmers, D., & Abraham, C. (2010). Strategies for Effective Dissemination of the Outcomes of Teaching and Learning Projects. *Journal of Higher Education Policy and Management, 32*(1), 55–67.

TeachThought.Com. (2022). *Why Every Teacher Needs a Professional Network.* https://www.teachthought.com/pedagogy/why-every-teacher-needs-a-professional-learning-network/.

Vygotsky, L. S. (1962). *Thought and Language.* MIT Press. https://doi.org/10.1037/11193-000

Wenger, E. (1998). *Communities of Practice: Learning, Meaning, and Identity.* New York: Cambridge University Press.

Writing the abstract
Jan Gourd

Once you get to this stage of your dissertation, you are nearly there.

This should be a great section to write in your dissertation, not least because you are nearly finished; all the hard work has been done, you now know what your outcomes are and this is your last job, to write as succinctly as possible an overview of the whole project. Abstracts are generally about 250–300 words long and they have to be written really succinctly to cover all the points you need to make.

What is an abstract?

An abstract is like an advertisement for your paper. You are showcasing the ideas and concepts that you have been working with. You are stating your methodology and your research question and you are summarising your findings. You are enticing the reader in but making sure that they know at the outset what they will find. In this point, it is not like a novel. You want the reader to know the ending but to be interested enough in the journey to read on.

An example

Abstract from a study looking at how to develop trainees' knowledge of pedagogical practices

'Developing pre-service teachers' (PSTs') knowledge of pedagogical practices can be particularly challenging within university classrooms. Teacher educators are well placed to provide PSTs with theoretical perspectives on pedagogical practices; what is particularly challenging, however, is linking theory with practice and developing PSTs' breadth and depth of knowledge in mathematical concepts. In this article, we describe the experiences undertaken by two cohorts of PSTs during their tutorials designed to assist them to notice and discuss Year 2 students' responses to an array task. Open-coding was used to analyse PSTs' selection and sequencing of five different work samples. Findings indicated that while the authentic work samples assisted the PSTs to make connections with the students' mathematical understandings, the lesson also provided an insight into the PSTs' own foundation knowledge of mathematical understandings relating to children's development of multiplicative thinking'

Livy et al. (2017 p. 18).

This abstract is from an article in **Mathematics Teacher Education & Development**

This abstract starts by talking **about the problem that the study seeks to investigate**. The problem is the difficulty of trying to teach teachers how to teach whilst in a university classroom. It is written as 'Developing pre-service teachers' (PSTs') knowledge of pedagogical practices can be particularly challenging within university classrooms' Livy et al. (2017 p. 18).

So it is written as a statement.

Task 1

Try to write your study area in a similar way; for example, if your study was on a specific practice in the EYFS, you could write something like this:

Teaching XXXX has often been seen as problematic amongst practitioners in early years classrooms.

Have a go for your study.

Our example then goes on to say that, although this is a problem, the tutors should be well placed to do this (probably as they have been doing this for years) but it then highlights a specific area that the authors have reflected on that is particularly problematic.

'Teacher educators are well placed to provide PSTs with theoretical perspectives on pedagogical practices; what is particularly challenging, however, is linking theory with practice and developing PSTs' breadth and depth of knowledge in mathematical concepts' (Livy et al., 2017, p. 18).

So if we were constructing an abstract for a study on a specific practice in early years, we might now be writing...

Teaching XXXX has often been seen as problematic amongst practitioners in early years classrooms. Early years practitioners are well placed to provide the resources needed to playfully investigate XXXX but often lack the specific skills to develop XXXX.

We are here locating the problem that we are seeking to investigate.

Where XXXX is music you might have.

Teaching music has often been seen as problematic amongst practitioners in early years classrooms. Early years practitioners are well placed to provide the resources needed to playfully investigate sounds but often lack the specific skills and knowledge to develop musicality.

So we are expanding on the initial problem.

Task 2

Try to expand on the initial statement that you have made about your study to include some elaboration of the original statement.

Our example abstract then highlights the methodology. We get to know who the research participants are (two cohorts of PSTs) and a bit about the method (during their tutorials to ...)

'In this article, we describe the experiences undertaken by two cohorts of PSTs during their tutorials designed to assist them to notice and discuss Year 2 students' responses to an array task' Livy et al. (2017 p. 18).

Now include a statement about the participants in your study and the methodology you have employed.

For example

Teaching music has often been seen as problematic amongst practitioners in early years classrooms. Early years practitioners are well placed to provide the resources needed to playfully investigate sounds but often lack the specific skills and knowledge to develop musicality. *This project, located within a constructivist paradigm, asked ten early years practitioners about their confidence in teaching music to children within a reception class in a mainstream school.*

Task 3

Now we begin to look at the analysis of the data collected through the methods used.

'Open-coding was used to analyse PSTs' selection and sequencing of five different work samples' (Livy et al., 2017 p. 18).
    So in our EY scenario, we could add:

Teaching music has often been seen as problematic amongst practitioners in early years classrooms. Early years practitioners are well placed to provide the resources needed to playfully investigate sounds but often lack the specific skills and knowledge to develop musicality. This project, located within a constructivist paradigm, asked ten early years practitioners about their confidence in teaching music to children within a reception class in a mainstream school. *Interviews were used to give the practitioners a voice to articulate the demands placed on them in regard to this curriculum area and their confidence in teaching it effectively. Transcripts from the interviews, coded thematically, showed ...*

Here you are letting the reader know that your specific method of data collection was interviews, and that in order to make sense of the data (analyse it), you used thematic coding.

So try adding a statement about the methods and analysis in your project.

Task 4

Finally, in our example abstract, we have a statement about the findings-;

> 'Findings indicated that while the authentic work samples assisted the PSTs to make connections with the students' mathematical understandings, the lesson also provided an insight into the PSTs' own foundation knowledge of mathematical understandings relating to children's development of multiplicative thinking' (Livy et al., 2017 p. 18).

So again in our EY example we could have

Teaching music has often been seen as problematic amongst practitioners in early years classrooms. Early years practitioners are well placed to provide the resources needed to playfully investigate sounds but often lack the specific skills and knowledge to develop musicality. This project, located within a constructivist paradigm, asked ten early years practitioners about their confidence in teaching music to children within a reception class in a mainstream school. Interviews were used to give the practitioners a voice to articulate the demands placed upon them in this curriculum area and their confidence in teaching it effectively. Transcripts from the interviews, coded thematically, showed *that only one of the ten practitioners felt comfortable planning musical activities and carrying these out.*

So, now add to your abstract the headline from your research.

This study highlights the lack of confidence that early years teachers have in delivering musical experiences to children and shows the need for more attention to be given to this area in pre-service and in-service training.

You then should have a fairly concise abstract that you can work on with your supervisor.

Task 5

In order to refine your own abstract, have a look at some of the following examples and ask yourself if from the abstract you can answer the following questions:

What is the study about?

Who are the participants?

What methods of data collection and analysis were used?

What did they find out?

If you can answer all these questions from an abstract, then it has served its purpose.

Further examples of abstracts

Play

'Previous research has indicated that the centrality of play within curricula documentation is not necessarily enough to guarantee its successful implementation, and that practice can be challenged by parental attitude, inadequate theoretical understanding and training, pressure to evidence learning outcomes and the availability of physical resources. This paper considers perceptions of play amongst 26 early years practitioners who are involved in delivery of the Foundation Phase in Wales, a recently-introduced curricular approach designed to foreground play. Using data collected via semi-structured questionnaires, practitioners reported limited knowledge and training in play, felt relatively under confident in defending play practice and continued to see curriculum objectives as being a barrier to their play practice. An additional challenge described by practitioners related to children's own play skills and ability. The findings raise issues for further consideration by policy makers in relation to training and resources. Other professionals might also benefit from shared insight into early years practitioners views, enabling them to appreciate and support the work of these professionals in their bid to provide the best educational experiences for every child' (Howard 2010, p. 91).

Childminders

The present study seeks to address the dearth of research focused on childminding (family day care or family childcare) in Ireland, despite its significant role in national childcare provision. One overarching aim was to explore childminders' cultural models of praxis and pedagogy in the Irish context. This research was conducted within the theoretical framework of Ecocultural Theory (ECT) (Weisner, 2002. 'Ecocultural Understanding of Children's Developmental Pathways', Human Development 1759: 275–281), referencing concepts in Attachment Theory, in the context of historical and current policy in Ireland, Europe and the US over the last 30 years. A mixed method approach was adopted using the Ecocultural Family Interview for Childminders (EFICh) protocol, which included holistic ratings, field notes, photographs taken by participants, and a case study survey. This article describes one cultural model identified among childminders in this study, a Close Relationship Model of praxis in a home-from-home environment, prioritising love and fun in mixed age childcare, developing enduring relationships in an extended childminding family. To effectively engage professional childminders in Ireland, any proposed system of regulation, support, and education should be aligned with this cultural model to maximise the benefits of childminding for children's outcomes in the twenty-first century.

(O'Regan et al., 2020, p. 675)

Hopefully, this task has allowed you to further analyse your own work.

SO RECAP – what should be included?

The first part of an abstract summarises the rationale but in the past tense. This is where your position at the outset will be important as the reader will judge the validity of your research in conjunction with this and in conjunction with the methodology and methods you chose. You then proceed to talk about the research process and finally the findings all in a succinct way.

Possible starting phrases for an abstract (just to get you going)

This study is important because…

This study looked at…

This study examined the role of…

This study was conducted to…

This study investigated the effects of…

This study addresses the impact of…

This study recognises the…

Summarise your key findings

Explain your methodology and methods clearly stating the participant sample.

Then, go onto the important part – the findings.

One of the main purposes here is to draw together your data and to write about what you found out. There will be many things that you find out. Some of these will hopefully be answers to your original questions but some will also be surprises. That's what makes research exciting, the finding out of something you weren't expecting.

How you presented your findings will depend upon the original question(s) and the methods that you used to gather and analyse your data. The way you present the findings should make the key messages obvious and easy to read.

Here, in the abstract, you are stating what you have found out. You should further highlight any implications for future practice and acknowledge any limitations.

So here is a checklist for you:

Does my abstract make my topic and context clear?

Am I making the objectives of my study clear?

Have I made the research design, data collection methods and modes of analysis transparent?

Have I provided the headline results?

Have I alluded to any surprises?

Have I finished with a comment on the significance of the research to future practice and or future research?

So now once you have written and checked your abstract, then you are finished. Well done.

References

Howard, J. (2010). Early Years Practitioners' Perceptions of Play: An Exploration of Theoretical Understanding, Planning and Involvement, Confidence and Barriers to Practice. *Educational & Child Psychology*, *27*(4), 91–102. https://doi.org/10.53841/bpsecp.2010.27.4.91.

Livy, S., Downton, A., & Muir, T. (2017). Developing Pre-Service Teachers' Knowledge for Teaching in the Early Years: Selecting and Sequencing. *Mathematics Teacher Education & Development*, *19*(3), 17–35.

O'Regan, M., Halpenny, A. M., & Hayes, N. (2020). Childminders' Close Relationship Model of Praxis: an Ecocultural Study in Ireland. *European Early Childhood Education Research Journal*, *28*(5), 675–689. https://doi.org/10.1080/1350293X.2020.1817239.

Staying sane
Jan Gourd

It is important when doing research to realise that there will be ups and downs. You must accept that there will be uncertainty, and you need to learn to live with that. This chapter is a collection of hints and tips to help you stay sane. There will be points where the work will 'flow' (Csikszentmihalyi 1990) and you will thrive, but there will undoubtedly be some other times where the pressure builds. We want to minimise these as much as possible.

In order to help you stay sane and be in control, then it is important that you:

Set realistic goals

The amount of time that you have for your research project as an undergraduate is generally going to be quite short. Usually, the research project runs through the third year of a degree programme and the academic year will start in late September. Also, generally, the completion or hand in date for projects tends to be sometime in April, so you have from September/October until April, a period of approximately six months. Also factor in your day job (if you have one), family and general life demands, then you will realise that this is not a long time.

Task 1

Make a timeline on a piece of paper. Put in the start date of your project/dissertation module and the hand in date.

Next add in a date that you are comfortable with to have the first draft finished. Leaving at least a week before, hand in to check it through for grammar and spelling errors, etc.

Add in the date by which your ethics form needs to be submitted. These are the dates that you have no control over, so they can be firmly written on the timeline.

Now the other events that you might like to put on the timeline are:

Complete the literature review.

Write up the rationale.

Write up the methodology.

Complete the fieldwork.

Data analysis time.

Results and conclusion written.

Write the abstract.

Meet with supervisor x4.

Write each of these on Post Its and put them on your timeline. This is where you do have some control; the Post Its can be moved but the timeline has fixed points that can't.

Be realistic and avoid Christmas and any other planned family events you know of and also work events that might take your time, e.g., Parents' evenings.

Take a look at your timeline and ask yourself how realistic it is. Maybe talk it through with a colleague or a fellow student. When you are happy with the position of the Post Its, then maybe commit that task to a permanent place on the timeline.

Take breaks

When you are working on a part of your project, you need to regularly take breaks and exercise and reward yourself. I am an ace procrastinator but once I get going, I have to set myself targets, sometimes that is about word count to be reached or chapters to be read. Sometimes I create a little Post It, maybe with the words in tickoffable amounts, e.g., 500 words complete, etc. Being able to see progress can be motivational as can promising yourself a break.

The above is obviously about breaks during the working period; however, it is also important to take calendar breaks around important family or social events and not feel guilty about it. This is why acknowledging these 'downtimes' is important within the timeline, as then they are scheduled and you can enjoy them guilt-free. Guilt is one of the worst parts of being a student for many mature and working people. Many mature students feel guilty about having to put this, their personal priority, over the needs of work and family. Therefore, be realistic and try to structure your project around these known events and other predictable stressors. Sometimes stressors and time eaters are not predictable, and some are also major life events, such as caring duties that we were unaware of at the outset of the project/dissertation. When these situations occur that you can do nothing about, then think about whether you should apply for an extension due to extenuating circumstances. If you do need to do this, you will probably need to fill out a form outlining what has happened to prevent you from submitting by the agreed deadline. You will probably also have to submit some evidence, such as General Practitioners' (GPs) note. Each university will have different procedures. You also need to email your supervisor, module lead and personal tutor as a matter of courtesy. If you need help, all universities have a student support team, who can guide you through difficulties and help with regulations and form filling. There are three things to remember. The first is that if you are in this situation you are not a failure. To get to the point of thinking about submitting this honours-level work is proof that you can do it. Secondly, if circumstances have prevented you from doing your best work, then you don't want to rush to submit something that is only half-finished or un-edited due to a lack of time. No one will want you to do that, and you won't get the grade you deserve, so again if there has been an unexpected circumstance, such as illness, that you couldn't do anything about, it is better to apply for an extension than to hand in an unpolished submission. Your supervisor would prefer that, as universities are judged on the performance of their students, you achieve the best grade that you are capable of. Thirdly, it is only an academic grade; whilst it is important, think about all the things in your life that are more important to you. You need to keep this in proportion and not make your own health worse by worrying about it. The thing to remember is to try to act as soon as you realise that you are slipping on your timeline.

Connect with others

During your course, you will hopefully have had time to bond with your fellow students. Hopefully, the social aspect has been important to you. Certainly, when I teach students who are working, they look forward to meeting together to discuss work dilemmas and sometimes even share their success stories. They have active online networks where they share their frustrations, and sometimes as lecturers, we too get frustrated by the navigated information that is shared on these networks, a bit like a whispering game where the meaning of an exchange between tutor and students is interpreted many times until there is little of the original message left! So a tip: if you are seeking an answer to an academic question, it is best to ask the tutor yourself! Aside from that, all forms of connecting with others will help you maintain your sanity.

The same is true of staying connected to those friends and family who have nothing to do with your course. It is important to recognise that your life has many parts, and all of these need to be nurtured to maintain a sense of well-being and belonging.

The dissertation or project can at times seem like a lonely endeavour though, because it is an individually chosen topic. This doesn't mean that you should work all the time on your own. Often, a study group can be a good way to stay connected. In our university, there are rooms that students can book in advance to work together. So how can you help each other? You could arrange a time to meet together to write silently; whilst this might seem silly, there is something motivational about sitting in a room together and working individually. The connection of being part of a shared endeavour.

Another way to connect with others is to attend events; sometimes universities hold conferences for students, especially for 'H'-level students, on topics that might help their studies. Whilst these are often optional and it is easy to say 'I don't really need to go to that', it will give you a chance to connect with others and sometimes a chance conversation or mention of a book can be just the thing to provide clarity to an issue you have been discussing in your project. Sometimes when you have been immersed in a project for a while, it can be hard to see the new angles or to clarify your thinking. Just meeting with like-minded people in an academic sense can be very worthwhile.

Task 2

Think about who your support network is at the moment. How do you connect now? Is that successful? As maybe through this project you will be in university less than previous years, how could you connect face-to-face if you wanted to?

Stay organised

The timeline suggestion in a previous chapter should help here, but you will need to take each of those tasks apart and break them down further. For example, with the literature review, you might have several smaller sub-target dates.

Keeping a note of all the sources and decisions you have made in a notebook will help you locate any important information later. Keep everything you write. Any chunks that you choose to delete from your work, don't; cut and paste them and save them in another document. Something that didn't seem important in the literature review that you delete might well become important when you are analysing your data or writing up your findings. Remember, in research, you must be prepared to be surprised. You cannot possibly know when you delete something in week two, whether it might be useful in the latter stages of the project/dissertation.

Try to keep your reference list as you go along, with the page numbers for any direct citation. This will save you so much time.

Also note when any library books are due back if your library still operates a timed loan system. I have had students run up substantial bills by becoming too absorbed in their projects and forgetting the mundane details of everyday academic life. Maybe add a different colour note to your timeline to remind you of any loan dates.

When you are writing, make sure that you also record the website addresses that you have used and make sure that you save the date that you last accessed them.

Websites are dynamic and subject to change, and what was there when you last looked might no longer be there when your work is marked. The date protects you by attributing the information to the site on the date you accessed it.

Also make sure that you have autosave on when you are working. Make sure that you use cloud-based storage or email yourself a copy of your work whenever you update it. I have lost count of the number of students who have lost substantial amounts of work through either forgetting to save after updating or having a computer crash sometimes beyond repair with the work being saved only on the hard drive. This happens frequently, so don't believe that it won't happen to you. Always, always keep a back-up.

Task 3

Make a list of your own organisational habits. Are they good or bad? How could you improve the efficiency of your work? Try to think of and commit to paper some resolutions that you will make. Don't make the list too extensive but concentrate on breaking bad habits that you know waste time; for example, do you always leave making a back-up copy of your work? If so, today and now would be a good time to break that bad habit. What else?

Stay healthy

It is important to not neglect yourself whilst working on your project. There is a temptation particularly when you are trying to meet deadlines to neglect the general healthy living principles that you generally employ. Food is my first example. You need to eat, and you need to eat for enjoyment as well as nutrition. The difficulty is the balance, and all too often when we are trying to create more time, we compromise and go for fast unhealthy food that needs little preparation. There are though many positives to taking time out to cook and enjoy a meal. If you have a family, you most likely don't have the option to compromise here, so in some ways, the extra responsibilities you have keep you grounded! The other thing you need to do is stay hydrated. Often when I am writing, I forget to drink enough and then I end up with a headache as the combination of screentime and dehydration takes its toll. I then, must, abandon the writing until the headache has gone and therefore have wasted potential time. I never learned this one, so this is a case of do what I say and not what I do! Maybe your bad habit when writing is to drink too much of the wrong stuff, such as coffee. Anyway, being aware of what you do is part of the solution, so think about how you can organise to stay healthy from a nutritional standpoint.

It is also important to maintain any exercise routines that you have. You can think through the next piece of writing whilst walking the dog; it isn't wasted time. The same goes for being at the gym, swimming, etc. Whilst there are some exercise habits that require your full attention – road cycling comes to mind – there are others that give your mind time and space to process new information and to synthesise this with existing knowledge.

You also need to keep your mind healthy and rationalise your worries about your project. You need to keep a sense of proportion and understand that all situations are generally retrievable. In universities, we talk about this at board meetings when we are looking at student profiles. If a student has missed an assignment or otherwise not completed something correctly, the first question asked is, how can this student retrieve this? No one wants you to fail, so if you are feeling overwhelmed, talk to your supervisor, your personal tutor, your programme lead or your module lead; just talk to someone as they can then signpost you to the remedy for your dilemma. Never feel that there isn't a solution; there always is; you just need to talk and maybe get help to find it.

So the main messages are:

Stay positive

There will be ups and downs throughout the project. Everyone experiences this. Think about all the students who have gone before and all those who will go after. They will get there, and so will you. You will finish the project, hand it in and graduate. Nothing lasts forever. In the final chapter, Marie talks about her experience of the dissi. Marie completed an Fda (the first year of her degree) in one institution, whereby she was in a small group but chose to do the third year or Top Up, which includes the 'dissi' with us and entered a much larger cohort. Marie's story is given in the next chapter. Since then, Marie has gone on to do a Master's and is now working on her PhD. You might also get hooked on research like she did! She emphasises seeking support to complete the balancing act of responsibilities that you likely have.

Seek support if you need it

From everyone, friends, families, colleagues, bosses, tutors, support services, library services, professional services, ICT services … everyone is there to help you.

Good luck and enjoy this experience.

Reference

Csikszentmihalyi, M. (1990). *Flow: The Psychology of Optimal Experience* (3rd ed.). Harper and Row.

A student journey

Marie Bradwell

Here Marie tells of her experience of her dissertation/project.

The undergrad dissi, the third year dissi, the DISSERTATION

These are my reflections of my experience, of my relationship with my undergraduate dissi and all the trimmings that go with this piece of work.

The build-up, the prep

I spent all summer reading, researching and thinking about my dissertation; I had my question, my topic and what I wanted to explore by the time September came around. I wished to look at the low wages that early years practitioners received and how this was or was not linked to the patriarchal systems and the links to the traditional roles of women; that if men were the higher percentage of the early years workforce, the pay would be higher. I read and made notes and explored my perceptions, my experiences and how this research could go ahead. Except that none of the reading or note-taking, or the thinking prepared me for the experience, nor did I use this as the focus of my dissi, my supervisor was not keen on the question.

Top tip: Know the area of focus, be familiar with the subject matter, perhaps you have written about this before. Ask to meet your supervisor before the summer break; this way the time can be used wisely to research the topic that has been discussed. AND your supervisor will be able to signpost some areas in order to support your reading.

The entrance

I entered the third year in a new institution after completing a foundation degree in a small (a four-student cohort) college. At the start of the year and the start of the dissi, experience was a full-day workshop full of words, such as primary and secondary research, library-based, quantitative, qualitative, ontology, epistemological and methodological approaches. I had no idea what any of these were or how they were relevant to my studies. My brain hurt, my feelings were that of anxiousness and this created the bodily reaction of shaking, being cold and crying. I had no idea what I was doing or how I would be able to complete what was being asked of me. I remember asking if primary or secondary research was easier, to be told they were both the same amount of work. I have since decided that for me, primary qualitative research is easier as this is person-based, not literary-based, and for me, more interesting.

If there is interest, there is motivation, which enables ease of process. Even so, I was wholly unprepared. The first week was so overwhelming with the information and the expectations, not only those placed, as I thought, by staff but those pressures I placed on myself also. I needed to achieve this; I could not abandon what I was trying to do. I was a role model for my children, a single parent setting an example, a single parent trying to increase the chances for my family, knowing I was needed as a breadwinner, carer and mother. The balance between being a full-time student, a full-time mom and a part-time worker is often known, but is not at the forefront in academic areas. All factors that need to be acknowledged in my journey of undertaking a dissi and crying.

Top tip: Buy and have lots of tissues at hand! Be kind to yourself and aware of all your roles and responsibilities that you have. Ensure that you advise your supervisor or staff member with whom you are comfortable at the university about your various roles and responsibilities. Become familiar with the terminology, not necessarily understanding all of these, just being familiar is a good starting point.

The structure

And then there was the layout of the dissi, the layout is a key point; get this right and instant marks are awarded. Again, this was introduced in the first week by lovely staff, but that did not matter. I did not understand how this was being introduced or why I could not get the IT component, the document on Word, to do what I needed it to do; or why I could not understand the commands that were clearly set out for us as students. I left the session in which this was being delivered, and I cried, and I cried. I went to the chaplaincy and cried, but later I did the structure on my own, and this took longer than it would have in the taught session. Through working on this in a step-by-step process, I accomplished the first step for my dissi. The structure was in place in a Word document. I could now add to this as my writing accumulated. A key step and one that is vital to accomplish at the beginning of the dissi journey.

Top tip: Persevere, believe that you can and there will be a way, perhaps a unique way, but there will be a way. Make use of all the resources available, including the support from non-academic staff, specifically those in IT services.

The supervisor

During the first part of the academic year, I received an email confirmation of who my supervisor would be. I was nervous; all the staff were new to me, and I was worried about if they would listen, what they would be like and if this lecturer would be supportive. Following the confirmation email, I sent an email to my supervisor to arrange an initial meeting. It was during this meeting that I was told the topic I had initially thought about would not be advisable. I was upset; I cried in the meeting; I had tried to hold these back, but I could not. There had been so much build-up to this point, and then nothing. I had to now consider if there was another option; there was; the 30-hour funding for childcare was a bill, and there were a lot of sector discussions around how this probable future policy would impact preschool and nursery settings. So, this became the focus of my dissertation – not my initial thought but an area that was still of interest to me and one that was much more in my comfort zone.

A supervisor's role is to support us and to ensure that what we do is to the best of our ability. For me, this was not taking on an area that at the time I did not know enough about. I had been upset about this, but looking back, to achieve what I was capable of, I needed an appropriate and accurate topic for me, my position, my current knowledge at the time and a question that was clear and concise. The question needed to be contemporary, one that could be researched within the time scale given, and in an area that I felt comfortable in. This is the benefit of an experienced supervisor; they can advise you on the feasibility of what you want your research to accomplish.

Throughout the academic year, I met with my supervisor on several occasions. I was aware that there is only a small number of allocated hours for this support, and in order to gain the most from the face-to-face sessions, these needed to be spread effectively across the timeframe. In addition, these needed to be requested by me in a timely fashion; I would email at least seven to ten days prior to requesting a meeting. Conversations between the student and supervisor are effectual; they did not always feel positive to me as a student but were always beneficial.

Top tip: Create a working relationship with your supervisor; there is a balance to be maintained between you; they are there to support you in your project, not to lead you through this. Remember your supervisor will most probably be marking your dissi, so listen to their advice!

Timeline

Nine months, the same length as pregnancy, is a phrase that was shared with my cohort. The dissi is like having a baby, you think about the dissi, you breathe the dissi and you live the dissi. And of course, you still must complete all the other assessments for the year, and balance home, work and student life. But the dissi is the culmination of the total study, so no pressure! I knew a timeline was imperative for me; if this went awry, I would be in trouble and the balance in my life would be impacted. My timeline started with the completion of the ethics form and finished with the hand-in date. I always set the hand-in date for two weeks before the actual hand-in, just in case. This is what my timeline looked like:

Ethics – November

Literature review and methodology

Chapter – 15th January (a date that was set by the university)

Data collection – January and start of February

Analysis – February

Write-up – discussion, conclusion, appendices, completion – 18th April – again set by the university

And it worked! I was worried at times that this would not be achievable, but with self-discipline, the plan worked.

Top tip: Know yourself and how you work. Prepare the timeline with awareness of your working methods. Make sure that the ethics is completed first and foremost as you can't start data collection until you have ethical clearance!

Writing, data collection, analysing and writing

The dissi contains parts – clearly set-out parts – and this feels like a nice order to me: the intro, the literature review, the methodology, the discussion and the conclusion. I worked out the word count for each of my sections, so I knew what I was aiming for. I used the content of my ethics form for the basis of my literature review and methodology chapters.

I read and read, and my literature review was a thematic literature review. The methodology chapter was a struggle for me; even though this is included in the ethics form, the words remained a mystery for me. Qualitative and interpretive, I could manage and feel confident, but the ontology and epistemology, no. I am not sure that at undergraduate level, we need to have complete comprehension of these two terms. And if the chapter was written, I was going to move to the next step – the data collection. I was nervous; the semi-structured interviews were all set with sector practitioners, and I suppose the first time of doing a new activity, there will always be nerves. I need not have been apprehensive as these went well; there should have been a higher number of interviews than occurred, but some settings did not reply, and others decided against taking part. Again, these are normal parts of research, and although these rejections rankled at the time, it is any proposed participant's right to say no. It is better if they say no straight away rather than withdraw at a later stage.

The collected data once transcribed needed analysis. I had spent several hours researching how I would do this. This analysis was an area that I wished to get right. As well as reading the research books I went to the library and looked at past dissis to see how others had analysed their data. This was probably one of the most useful activities I undertook. The chance to see how others had analysed data, not only the method of analysis, but how this had then been displayed, set out for the reader, was incredibly beneficial. And I found my analysis a friendly thematic analysis. The themes that were produced provided structure for my discussion chapter and provided straightforward links with my literature review. The analysis, having been accomplished by hand, without using programs, had provided me with a real depth of knowledge of my data, so whilst writing up the discussion chapter, I knew exactly which data quotes to use and the similarities and the differences in the opinions; I heard the voices of the participants. Having this experience, the deep knowledge of data I believe supported my writing and the cohesiveness of the dissi.

Top tip: Know the type of literature review you are writing; do not worry if there are parts around the methodology that are still confusing – that is normal. Have a look at previous dissis so you can see how these are laid out; see the many ways of analysis and the structure of the main body and the appendices. Find the approach that fits well with you as a researcher.

Waiting and waiting

After the hand-in, there is the wait. Not only the wait for the dissi mark, but the wait for the overall mark for your degree. The mark that places you in first, 2:1 or 2:2. The wait felt like a long time, and then when the email came through to say that the overall marks were now available, this felt too soon. But look, read the email, make sure you look and do not keep waiting.

Top tip: Remember all you have accomplished to get to where you are now. The balancing is worth it, onwards to graduation.

Index

Note: **Bold** page numbers refer to tables and *italic* page numbers refer to figures.

abstracts, writing: checklist 110–111; childminders 109; data analysis 107–108; definition 105; expanding on the initial statement 107; findings 108, 110; play 109; pre-service teachers' (PSTs') knowledge, pedagogical practices 105–108; refining 108; starting phrases 110; writing the study area 106–107
academic books 61
academic malpractice 70
AI software 14–15
Archer, Margaret 14
artwork 41
authenticity 88, **88**
auto/biographical approaches 50

Barrow, C 66
bead collage activity 100–101
Booth, W. 65
Braun, V. 85
The British Educational Research Association (BERA) 47–48
The British Psychological Association 47
The British Sociological Association 47
Brookes, R. 36

Catchphrase (TV gameshow) 85
ChatGPT 14–15
child engagement 41
childminders 109

choosing a subject 4; AI software 14–15; deciding on the area of study 9; development 7–8; early years policy 5–7; mind mapping 13; moving on the area of study 9–12; play 7; possible areas of interest 4–5; professionalism 8; rationale 15–16; social conditions 8; welfare 8; working title 12–13
Clark, A. 34, 41
Clarke, V. 85
Clark, T. 85
closed-ended questionnaire 35
Cloud storage 71
Cohen, L. 40, 41
colour coding 88
combination questionnaire 35–36
conference presentations 97–98
confusion 89
constructivist paradigm 107, 108
content analysis 86
Corbett-Whittier, C. 74, 77, 78
COVID pandemic 55
Criminal Records Board 74
critical evaluation 67–69
critical thinking 18
Curtin, A. 8

data analysis: authenticity 88, **88**; colour coding 88; confusion 89; content analysis 86; discourse analysis 86; grounded analysis 86; interpretative

123

phenomenological analysis (IPA) 87; narrative analysis 86; qualitative data 85; quantitative data 87; research analysis 84, 85; statistical approach 31; suitable analysis method **87**, 88; systematic approach 85; thematic analysis technique 85; transparency 89; trustworthiness 88, **88**, 89; types of 85–87

data collection 31, 73; checklist 76–77; data storage 77; desk-based dissertations/projects 82–83; documents as data 81–82; dress code 80–81; ethical considerations 30–31; handling the data 74; high-quality data 73; interviews 77–79; management 80; methods 99–103; observation 75–77; permissions 73–74; questionnaires 79–80; visiting a setting 81

data storage 77

Dawson, C. 31

Declaration of Helsinki 1964 45

description evaluation 67–69

desk-based dissertations/projects 82–83

development 7–8

discourse analysis 86

dissemination 91; conference presentations 97–98; directive 93; formal outputs 91; formal ways 96; guidelines regarding publication 54–55; informal ways 94–96; magazine publications 99; method 93; poster presentations 98–99; training sessions 96–97; transfer of information 93; transfer of knowledge 93

dissertation/projects: analysing and writing 121; anxiousness 119; build-up 118; data collection 122; desk-based 82–83; entering the third year 118–119; the layout 119; simple research design 2; student–supervisor relationship 18–19; supervisor 118, 120; timeline 1, 120–121; transformative stage 94; waiting for marks 122; *see also individual entries*

Eames, V. 86

early years education 2

Early Years Foundation Stage (EYFS) 5–7, 82–83

early years policy 5–7

Ecocultural Family Interview for Childminders (EFICh) protocol 109

Ecocultural Theory (ECT) 109

Elliott, V. 75, 80

epistemology 33

ethical approval: avoiding plagiarism 54; balance of power 46–48; concepts 48; consent of participants 49–50; data storage 52–53; disclosure 53; educational research 46–48; ethical complexities 45; guidelines 48; harm 51–52; incentives 51; privacy 52–53; reasons for 44–45; recognition of individual identity 48–49; responsibilities for publication 54–55; responsibilities for researchers' well-being and development 55; responsibilities to sponsors, clients and stakeholders 53; responsibilities to the community of educational researchers 54; right to withdraw 50–51; safeguarding 53; transparency 51

ethnographic paradigmatic approach 99–100

European Early Childhood Education Research Association (EECERA) 44, 47

Evans, J. 47, 76

face-to-face sessions 120

Fejes, Andreas 14

Firth, J. 92

'five Ws' 31

formal dissemination 96

General Data Protection Regulations 52–53

Google Forms 36

Google Scholar 62

Gregory 85

Grey literature 62

grounded analysis 86

Guba, E. G. 88

Hall, K. 8, 42
Hamilton, L. 74, 77, 78
Harvey, David 14
Hey, C. 75
Howells 85

impact 92–93
informal dissemination 94–96
Ingram, J. 75, 80
interpretative phenomenological analysis (IPA) 87
interviews 77–79, 107; artefact or images 38; planning 38–39; setting up and preparation 38–39; stimulated recall interview 38; types 37; writing up 39
investigative approach 102

Jesson, J. K. 67, 69
journal articles 61–62

knowledge acquisition 92
Koshy, V. 34

Lee, A. 17
library database 59
Likert-style questions 34
Lincoln, Y. 88
Listening to Young Children (Clark) 41
literature review: academic malpractice 70; academic tone 69–70; description *versus* critical evaluation 67–69; locating sources 59–60; material management 64–65; note-taking system 66; overcoming writer's block 70–71; plagiarism 70; planning 58; purpose of 57; recording your reading 65; saving work 71; source quality 63–64; starting to write 57–58; structuring the chapters 66–67; time organisation 58; types of sources 60–63
Livy, S. 106

Mack, L. 89
magazine publications 99
McNiff, J. 93

methodology and methods: definition 30; gathering evidence, documents 41–42; interviews (*see* interviews); observations 39–41; ontological position 32–33; questionnaires (*see* questionnaires); sample 33; supervisors and choosing 30–32
Milner, Alison 100–101
mind mapping 13
mosaic approach 100
Moss, P. 2, 41
multiple in-text references 68–69
music teaching 107, 108

narrative analysis 86
neoliberal ideology 2
neo-liberal ideology 6
neo-liberalism 14
Nind, M. 8, 36
non-participant observation 40, 75
Nuremberg Code 1948 45

Oates, R. 75
observations 39–41, 75–77
O'Leary, Z. 67
online forums 97
ontology 32–33
open-ended questionnaires 35
opt-in/opt-out research 50
output, definition 92
Owens, Patrick 101–102

Papatheodorou, T. 50–51, 54, 75
paraphrasing 68
participant observations 40, 75–76
photographs 41
plagiarism 70
play 7, 109
Plowden Report (1969) 6
popular media coverage 63
poster presentations 98–99
pre-service teachers' (PSTs') knowledge 105–108
professionalism 8

qualitative data 30–31, 85
quantitative data 30–31, 87, 102

questionnaires 31, 33, 79–80; online tools 36; planning 34; type of participants/sample 34; types 35; uses 36–37

recommendations and conclusions: conference presentations 97–98; data collection methods 99–103; dissemination 91, 93; formal dissemination 96; impact 92–93; informal dissemination 94–96; magazine publications 99; output 92; poster presentations 98–99; showcasing the voices of my participants 94; training sessions 96–97
research analysis 84, 85
Research Gate 62
Research Methods for Understanding Professional Learning (Hall and Wall) 42
Ritchie, J. 92
Robertson, Susan 14
Rogers, S. 47, 76

Sahlberg, Pasi 14
Savin-Baden, M. 6, 80
scanning 64–65
search engine 59
semi-structured interviews 37, 38; *see also* interviews
shopping list approach 66
skimming 64
'smiley faces'/emojis 34
Smith, J. 39
Smith, S. 91, 92
social conditions 8
social media 36, 49
Spaces to Play (Clark and Moss) 41
Spencer, L. 92
staff meetings 96
stimulated recall interview 38
structured interviews 37
student support team 114
supervisor: achievement hopes with the research 20; advantages of working with 29; aims of meeting with 19–21; applying for an extension 114;

approaches to 17; being proactive 24; critical thinking 18; data analysis 84; dissertation/project 118, 120; engaging in discussion 24–25; expectations 20–23; getting the most out of 24–27; getting to know 19–20; having an open mind 26; holistic nature of 17; issues management 27, **27–28**; making notes 25–26; meeting deadlines 26; meeting organiser 26–27; plan emergence 20; reading 25; recording meetings 25–26; reflection 25; respond to/act on feedback 26; responsibilities **22–23**; scheduling next meeting/contact 20–21; self-awareness 24; supervision process 17; two-way communication relationship 89
Survey Monkey 36
systematic literature review 5

thematic analysis technique 85
Tombs, G. 6, 80
training sessions 96–97
transparency 89
triangulation 39–40
trustworthiness 88, **88**, 89

uncertainty handling in research: connecting with others 114–115; positiveness 117; seeking support 117; setting realistic goals 112–113; staying healthy 116–117; staying organised 115–116; taking breaks 113–114
United Nations Convention on the Rights of the Child (UNCRC) 50
university conferences 115
unstructured interviews 37

Walker, D. 91
Wall, K. 42
welfare 8
Westrup, R. 66
Wisker, G. 27
Wood, P. 39
work–life balance 4
workplace posters 99

For Product Safety Concerns and Information please contact our EU representative GPSR@taylorandfrancis.com
Taylor & Francis Verlag GmbH, Kaufingerstraße 24, 80331 München, Germany